"We Will Remember Them"

The Bidford Fallen of The Great War

by

Bob Marshall

Co-authors Paul Clarke, Wendy and Mark Shaddick

Published by Bidford Publications

"We Will Remember Them"

Copyright © Bidford and District History Society

All rights reserved. No part of this publication may be reproduced, distributed, or transmitted in any form or by any means, including photocopying, recording, or other electronic or mechanical methods, without the prior written permission of the publisher, except in the case of brief quotations embodied in critical reviews and certain other noncommercial uses permitted by copyright law.
For permission requests, write to the publisher,
addressed "Attention: Permissions Coordinator," at the address below.

Bidford and District History Society
Church House, Church Street, Bidford-on-Avon, Alcester, B50 4DA

Published by Bidford Publications
2014

ISBN 978-0-9575790-1-9

Designed by Chris Wheeler Graphic Design: www.chriswheeler.co.uk

Printed by CPI Antony Rowe: www. cpibooks.co.uk

Foreword

The Great War is aptly named. It was greater in scale, cost, and consequences than any previous conflict. It shattered empires, created new nation states, and resulted in lasting changes to British, European and world society.

Its battles too were greater than any that had been seen before. The first day of the Battle of the Somme cost the British Army almost 60,000 men killed, wounded and missing. Grasping the sheer scale of loss is almost impossible. A particularly arresting method may be employed when attending a popular sporting event - glance around the stadium, and imagine that all of the spectators (and perhaps more) would have fallen in a single day. It is this scale, constantly reinforced by the sight of the many war memorials dotted around the country, which gives the war its lingering sense of tragedy.

In recent years historians have done much to advance our understanding of how and why battles were fought in the Great War. The latest scholarship has taken the study of the war beyond the notorious first day of the Somme and illustrated how the British Army evolved into a war-winning force by 1918. Yet, there is a need for balance in this assessment. In studying the victories of the British Army we can sometimes forget that even successful battles came at a high cost in lives - and defeats even more so. Fortunately, there is a growing body of excellent literature dedicated to the individual stories of the war. The book you currently hold is a perfect example.

"We Will Remember Them"

This is a concise, beautifully illustrated and deeply touching volume. The diverse experiences and backgrounds of the men in this book remind us of the broad nature of the British Army. There are pre-war regulars and wartime volunteers, most young, but some surprisingly old. Although the majority fell on the Western Front there are also casualties from the Middle East and Salonika. What unites them is their humanity: when reading about their backgrounds and families we are reminded that each life lost in war is an individual tragedy.

The study of war is a complex art that takes place on many levels. Academics naturally gravitate towards the 'big picture', but we are lucky to have books such as this one to remind us that armies are not monolithic, unthinking organisations, but are instead composed of a multitude of individuals, each with their own story to tell.

Dr. Spencer Jones
Senior Lecturer in Armed Forces and War Studies
University of Wolverhampton

Acknowledgements

The authors would like to thank the following for their valuable contributions to this book: Lorna Edwards and Jane Crompton for proof reading; Roger Leese, chairman of the Research Group, for his constant encouragement and for reading the second draft; Sandra Parker who discovered the parish magazines containing letters from soldiers from Bidford fighting in the Boer War and for her photography work; Rodney Crompton for photography work and also Major Bob Woodford of the Grenadier Guards for his assistance in researching the records of George Oakey.

The authors express thanks to the following
for their kind permission to use copyright material:
The Evesham Journal
The Commonwealth War Graves Commission
Warwickshire County Record Office

Photographs

Every effort has been made to trace the copyright holders but the authors apologise if any inadvertent omission has been made. The owners of the collections referenced below have all granted permission for their photographs and postcards to be used.

Unless otherwise indicated, all photographs are from the Bob Marshall Collection.

The Rodney Crompton Collection
Mrs Doreen Byrd
Tony Bolton
The late Mona Arrowsmith
The late Joan McCrorie
The late Mac Freeman
The Irene Williams Collection
Pierre Vandervelden, Peruwelz, Belgium
Molly Henderson
The Evesham Journal
Don Mayrick
The late Alan Mumford
The late Minnie Ash
The late Minnie Seymour
The late Nan Wesson
Mick McCann, British War Graves.
Robert McCrorie
Hazel Mumford

"We Will Remember Them"

This book would not have been possible without financial assistance from the following sources, for which the authors are most grateful:

Bidford & District History Society	Bidford Parish Council
Bidford Community Group	Two Anonymous Donors
Emma March	Steven Holloway
Gordon's Butchers	Hall Reynolds
B.P.S. Bidford	Bidford MOT (Hew Lewis)
Bidford Hardware	

Warwickshire Young Firefighters, Bidford Branch

Bidford Fire Crew Social Fund	Peter Dickinson, Estate Agents
Mike Franklin	Colin Harris (Chemist) Ltd
Village Stores, Mickleton	Peter and Libby Batacanin
Julie Marshall	

CONTENTS

Page No.

Foreword
Acknowledgements

Contents

Prelude:
The Boer War: 1899-1902   *3*
Bidford and the First World War - Introduction   *13*
Chapter 2:
The Way They Were - Life in Bidford on the Eve of War   *15*
Chapter 3:
The Soldiers' Stories 1914   *19*
The Soldiers' Stories 1915   *23*
The Soldiers' Stories 1916   *53*
The Soldiers' Stories 1917   *79*
The Soldiers' Stories 1918-22   *115*
Keep the Home Fires Burning   *149*
The Armistice   *157*
Conclusion   *158*
Known Bidford Survivors   *163*
Statistics of the Fallen   *166*
Bibliography   *170*
Index   *171*

"We Will Remember Them"

37th R.A. howitzer battery going to Maddox Hill to throw lyddite into the Boer Laager, S. Africa

Library of Congress Prints and Photographs Division Washington, D.C. 20540 USA

Prelude:

The Boer War: 1899-1902

*"Great interest and anxiety are felt here as elsewhere in regard
to the news from the war in South Africa.
The number of our soldiers from this parish
who are at the front is very considerable and we are all anxious
to know of their welfare and safety
in this long and sanguinary struggle."*

So wrote the vicar of Bidford, the Reverend Alfred Evans, in the parish magazine of February 1900 about the soldiers from the parish serving in what is now known as the Boer War.

Tension between South Africa (then part of the British Empire) and the neighbouring Boer states of the Transvaal and Orange Free State over territorial rights, had led to the invasion of British territory by a Boer army in October 1899 and, by December, to the astonishment of the rest of the world, the Boers had defeated British troops and the towns of Ladysmith, Mafeking and Kimberley were besieged. The concern expressed by the Reverend Evans came just after the disastrous defeat of British forces at Spion Kop in January 1900 when 1,200 were killed or wounded in one of the worst defeats suffered by the British army since the Crimean War. The next morning the Boers took photographs of the British dead on the battlefield and these were published throughout the world.[1] Reinforcements were speedily sent out, along with General Roberts, to take command. Queen Victoria voiced the mood of the nation - "We are not interested in the possibilities of defeat; they do not exist".[2]

In March 1900 the parish magazine published a list of soldiers from Bidford fighting in

---

1. A. N. Wilson, 'The Victorians'
2. Ensor, 'England, 1870-1914'

"We Will Remember Them"

South Africa as they "especially need our prayers that they be preserved from harm".

- C. Wilkes (Driver) O Battery Royal H.A. Regular
- J. B. Chambers (Trooper) D Troop, 2nd Life Guards (Regular)
- H. Sheaf (Private) B. Company, 2nd North Staffordshires (Reserve)
- A Spittle (Private) 2nd Duke of Cornwall's Light Infantry Company (Reserve)
- P. Locke (Private) 2nd Duke of Cornwall's Light Infantry Co. (Reserve)
- Ben Freeman (Private) 2nd Royal Warwickshires (Reserve)
- Frank Freeman (Private) 2nd Royal Warwickshires (Regular)
- Harry Hancock (Private) King's Royal Rifles , C Company (Regular)
- J. Quiney (Driver) Royal Horse Artillery (Regular)
- Phil Nutting (Private) Loyal North Lancs (Reserve)
- Eli Bennett (Private) E Company, 2nd Cameronians (Reserve)
- G. Harris (Private) Oxford Light Infantry (Regular)
- T. Harris (Private) 2nd Coldstream Guards (Reserve)
- Denis Wilkes (Corporal) 14th Hussars (Regular)
- Ernest Gardner (Private) Coldstream Guards (Regular)
- Harry Wilcox (Shoeing Smith) 37th Howitzer Battery (Regular)
- George Vale (Colour Sergeant) Royal Welch Fusiliers (Regular)
- E. Kingzett (Corporal) 2nd Imperial Warwickshire Yeomanry (Volunteer)
- H Gardner (Private) E. Company 1st York and Lancaster (Reserve)
- T Wesson (Private) King's Royal Rifles (Regular)
- Reg Tipping (Private) G. Company, Imperial Light (Volunteer)

Twenty one soldiers was a remarkably high number for a village with a population of around 1,500 and at least three of these went on to fight in the 1914-18 conflict and also survived (Thomas Harris, Paddy (Henry) Locke and Phil Nutting). Perhaps lack of employment opportunities other than agricultural work led to some of these young men joining the armed services which, at the end of the 19th century, were so much larger with an empire to defend. The village was determined to show its support for its servicemen and the parish magazine of December 1899 recorded that: "A very good collection of money has been made in Bidford in aid of the Soldiers' and Sailors' Families Association. Great interest and sympathy is felt throughout the parish, a great many families have relations and friends at the front. A house to house collection was

The Boer War: 1899-1902

made….resulting in £14. 1s.7d… A special sermon was preached in the evening by the vicar at the parish church. 'God Save the Queen' and special hymns were heartily sung by the choir and a large congregation."

The unquestioning support for the war nationwide and the popular belief in Britain's imperial supremacy was no better exemplified than in the sentiments expressed at the annual supper held in Bidford in January 1900 of the United Patriots National Benefit Society, as reported in the Evesham Journal. Formed in 1843 as a society providing cheap insurance for its members, the Bidford branch had been in existence since 1870 and had a membership of 251 adults and 79 juveniles. Its stated aim, "to maintain the supremacy of our country and our flag"[3], perhaps mirrors the way British people thought at the beginning of the 20th century; an approach to life which would explain people's reactions to the outbreak of war in 1914 and which would be changed forever by that conflict. The Evesham Journal reported that:

"One of Bidford's most gratifying characteristics is its numerous societies for the cultivation of thrift… The local branch of the United Patriots National Benefit Society, which, by the way, is the largest in the Birmingham district, can fairly claim to be the most prosperous…The annual winter gathering which takes the form of a supper, was held at the headquarters (the Mason's Arms Inn) on Monday evening… Dr G. H. Fosbroke genially presided over numerous company. … A capital supper was served by Mrs Holder. The chairman gave the loyal toasts, remarking that they all rejoiced in having Her Majesty reigning over them at the beginning of this century. He alluded in eulogistic terms to the prosperity of the country under Her Majesty's rule and he observed that, although it had been said it had been a reign of wars, he considered the whole of them to be just wars."[4]

Such certainty at the dawn of a new century was to be cruelly shattered 14 years later and Dr Fosbroke himself would lose his grandson in the mud and horror of the trenches. Their unbowed optimism was also expressed ("…after a verse of the National Anthem being heartily sung") by the secretary, Mr E. A. Wilson of Bell Court who commented on the defeats recently suffered at the hands of the Boers as being : "…not exactly defeat but they (the British army) had been repulsed for the time being…" He was, however, sure that: "the tide of battle and fortune would turn and then not only would this bravery be applauded by the world… but this crisis had shown that everyone

---

3. Evesham Journal, 6th January 1900

4. Ibid

who had British blood running through his veins, whether in Australia, Canada or wherever he might be, felt proud to be a subject of that gracious Queen. …The time would come when the Boers would have to meet the British cold steel and then a different tale would be told".[5]

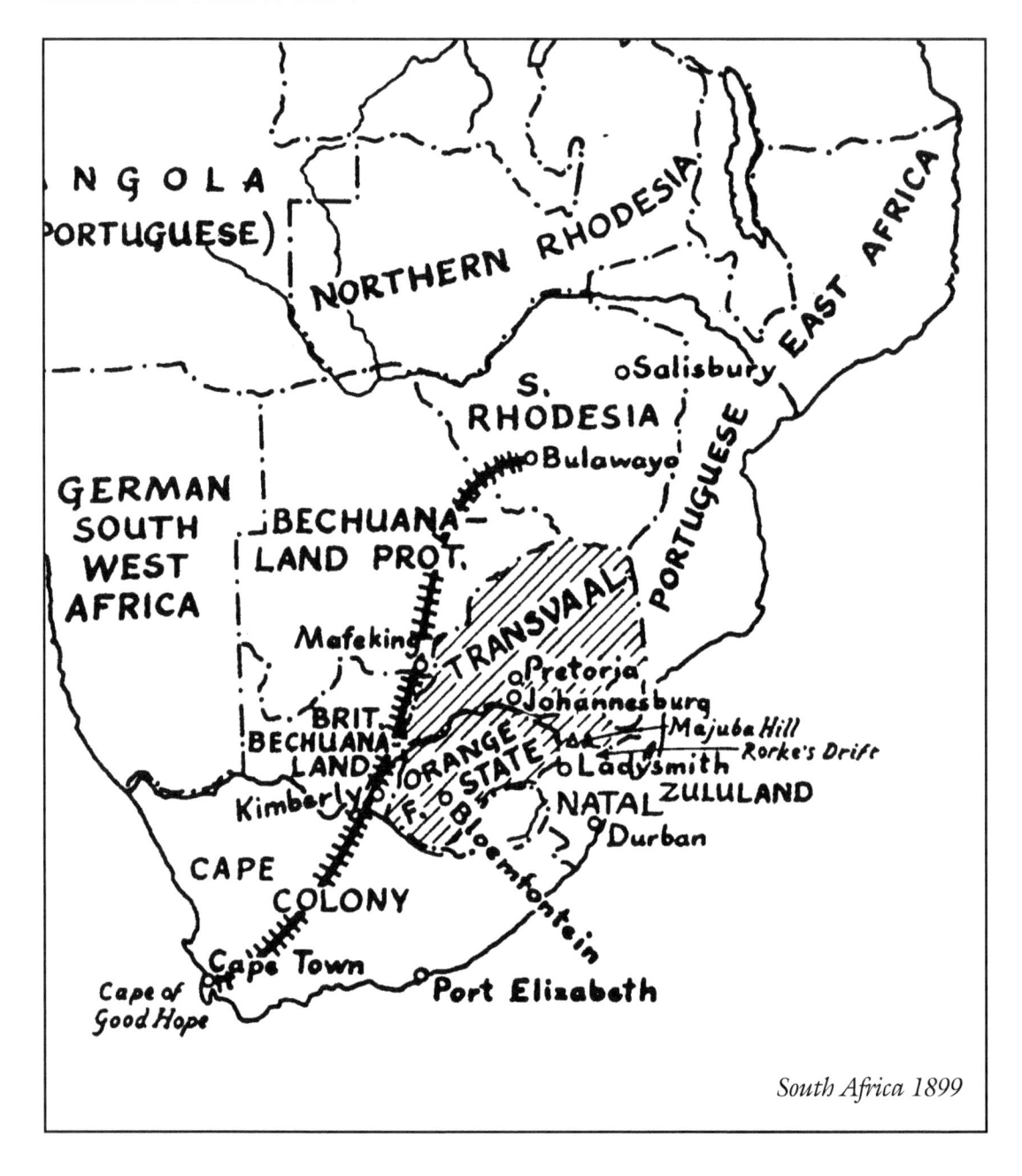

South Africa 1899

The Boer War: 1899-1902

The Turn of the Tide

During 1900, General Roberts began reversing the defeats suffered by the British. On 27th February the relief of Ladysmith, which had been besieged since 1899, was celebrated in the village, as reported in the Evesham Journal: *"The news was received in Bidford at 10.05 and caused great rejoicing. Numbers of flags were soon flying including the Union Jack upon the church tower. The bells rang forth merrily in the evening and in the usual Bidford fashion the event was celebrated by a dinner at the White Lion Hotel in the evening. Mr presided."*[6]

The parish magazine of May 1900 recorded in the Annual General Meeting accounts that 12 shillings was paid to all the bell ringers for a special peal to celebrate the relief of Ladysmith.

The relief of Mafeking in May 1900, where Robert Baden Powell had held out for 217 days, caused wild rejoicing throughout the country and the June parish magazine accounts record that Bidford joined in the celebrations: *"Subscription for celebrating the relief of Mafeking, Saturday May 19th 1900. Giving all children in Bidford parish a tea and river trip to Cleeve, followed by sports and torchlight procession."*

The gifts sent to Bidford soldiers using the funds collected were clearly appreciated and the June 1900 magazine published letters of thanks from some of them. It would appear that there was no censorship as they give a wonderful account of the Boer War from the soldiers' points of view, highlighting especially the privations they suffered as well as the resourcefulness and determination of their Boer opponents.

On March 29th 1900 Albert Spittle wrote from Bloemfontein: *"It is with great pleasure I take up the pen to thank you and my many well-wishers for their very acceptable gift, which, I am very pleased to say, was placed in my hands this morning. The tobacco was more than pleasingly acceptable, owing to the fact that of late we haven't been able to get the above article. Cigarettes here are nineteen pence a box of ten, so you can understand what even the slightest gift of the above means. …I cannot, in words, express how I feel for being the recipient of unexpected kindness, and it makes one feel glad when knowing that, although thousands of miles away, there*

6. Evesham Journal, March 1900

are many who have us in their hearts and minds." He went on to describe a battle he had taken part in on Sunday 18th February at Paardeberg. *"We arrived at about 2 o'clock in the morning, coming directly under fire and witnessing some of the most accurate shooting on the part of our artillery… the Boer Laager and convoy speedily being set ablaze. Shortly after, under the command of our colonel, we waded across the river; by Jove! This was a feat, we having to hold on to a rope like grim death, loosing meaning certain death, for the torrent was running quite ten miles an hour. This successfully accomplished, it wasn't long ere bullets were spitting all around us, doctors and stretcher bearers being now called for in all parts of the field. Our Colonel, plucky little fellow, bravest of us all, when we got close enough gave the order to "Charge". He was scorning all danger, bravely leading us on, but hardly had the above order left his lips before he was shot down…We charged twice but to no purpose, nothing could possibly outlive such shooting. We lost heavily, Colonel, Adjutant, one Captain killed, four Lieutenants wounded, and ninety six men killed and wounded. This is a heavy total considering the short time it took place in. No doubt, when dusk fell, both the enemy and ourselves were glad of a respite. …Our journey back to camp ground, a good distance, was made uncomfortable by our clothes being completely soaked, but withal one was pleased to think that we were spared to take part in this. The following days were devoted to shelling the Boer position, convoy and entrenchments; and on Shrove Tuesday… Cronje and his force of between four and five thousand unconditionally surrendered... We shall all of us be right well pleased when the war is brought to a successful conclusion and we on the road home to re-join those anxiously waiting to welcome us. Perhaps that is not far distant."*

Ben Freeman wrote from Bloemfontein on the same day: *"Just a few lines in answer to your kind and welcome letter, and also to thank you for the parcel which I got quite safe about two hours ago, and can assure you it was a real Godsend, for since we marched into this place we have had nothing to smoke but Boer tobacco, and dried tea leaves sometimes and they both taste about the same. Kindly thank the people of Bidford for me for the luxury I have received from them."* He had also been to Paardeberg but after Albert Spittle and he described in darker tones the aftermath of the battle there. *"It was by the side of a river and the sights we had to look at were enough to make your blood run cold. No doubt Lord Roberts had been paying them out for the death of his son with a vengeance. There were hundreds of wagons in the laager and from the way he had bombarded and fired them, there was not a vestage (sic) of woodwork left, only the tyres of the wheels and just the axle irons. Thousands of rifle barrels and burst ammunition lay scattered everywhere, and talk about mules, oxen and transport animals, the river was full of them, and to make it worse it was the only water we could get to wet our thirsty whistles with and some days we*

The Boer War: 1899-1902

were on half rations of bully beef and biscuits".

What Freeman did not know was that Roberts had offered safe passage to the women and children in the town but this had been refused by Cronje, the Boer general.

On April 1st J Quiney wrote from Bloemfontein: *"I now take the pleasure of writing to you to acknowledge the receipt of your splendid and useful present, which you and the inhabitants of Bidford have been so kind in sending out to me… I feel highly honoured to think that I am one of the representatives of the good old town of Bidford, I can assure you that a bit of tobacco is a great comfort to me out here. We have been on the march now for several weeks and we could not get any tobacco, and we have even smoked for a substitute tea leaves and coffee grounds…We had a big fight at Colesburg on New Year's Day, that was the first time I had been in action, and none can realise what it is to hear the shells come screaming over you and hear the bullets pinging around you. I felt a bit queer for a time, but have got used to it now, as I have been in action dozens of times since and long Tom is a friend of mine. It is a large gun with a long range, and it throws a heavy shell, but its bursting capacity is rotten, and it has been a good thing for us that it is so, as we have often had to go within rifle-shot to shift them from their formidable positions. I must tell you that I have had the pleasure of taking part in the relief of Kimberley, we had a big fight the day we relieved it – we had a grand artillery duel and silenced their guns and then the cavalry made a splendid charge and routed them, it was a sight worth seeing. I am sorry to say that we had a loss of about 8 killed and 30 wounded and we lost a great many horses. We had the honour of marching through the town first, amid great enthusiasm from its brave defenders. We only stayed one day, and then continued our march towards Bloemfontein: we took great part in capturing Cronje and his forces, he made a good stand, but was forced to surrender, or come out of his entrenchments and fight, no doubt if he had done so, we should have killed them all. We were forced to camp there on account of the exhausted condition of our horses. We had no corn for them, and no rations for ourselves: and we had to exist for over 2 weeks on less than quarter rations and we had to go out and graze our horses. You see we had been pushing on so fast that the supply column was a long way behind. We left there and marched on to Bloemfontein: we had several engagements with the enemy, and were expecting a big battle here but they evacuated early in the morning and we marched in at noon without any opposition. We are having a well-earned rest. We have been under the splendid command of Lord Roberts and General French, and we have been doing some of his Kandahar marches, with as you know splendid results. We had a splendid address read out to us from Lord Roberts, thanking us for the excellent way we had conducted ourselves under such privations and he said no troops could possibly do better. We shall get new issues of clothing and also a lot of fresh horses before we go any farther: we are all in rags and the horses are worn out. We have a bit of trouble from the enemy now and then but we don't fear much danger from them. We have captured a lot of prisoners and keep bringing them in daily. … Now I must draw to a close, hoping for a speedy close of the war and a safe return to dear old home."*

T. Wesson wrote from the Royal Rifles Field Force on April 20th: *"I must write these few lines to you, hoping to find you in the best of health and also the inhabitants of Bidford… and telling you that I have received the presents you sent me all right and safe and telling you that I am very pleased with them, and should have written to you before but being on the move I have not had time".*

Harry Wilcox was also very grateful for the gifts: *"I must give my best thanks to you who so kindly thought of us out here. I am most pleased with the articles you have sent, as they are very comfortable and useful; and the pipes, tobacco and cigarettes were very acceptable as I was fairly on the rocks for the want of a smoke".*

No one captured the grim reality of the war better than Phil Nutting: *"As you say in your letter, it is a terrible war, and there are lots of hardships, but we stand them without a murmur. I am sure nobody knows what we have to put up with, unless they have been in battle. It is not like fighting natives, for a native will face you, but these Boers get behind rocks and hills and we cannot get a chance at them."* His health had suffered as *"I must tell you that I have been in Kimberley all through the siege and we have had a very hard time of it. I am still at Kimberley, but in Hospital with dysentery. I am getting better now but it is a bad complaint; do not tell my parents as it will upset them".*

T. Harris of the Coldstream Guards was also pleased with the gifts: *"… more so by it coming from my own native place and by the way the funds were raised. I am sure it gives one courage and happiness to think one still has friends at home who are thinking about you. For I can assure you although my time has been so much occupied out here, my thoughts have often been at home among my friends; but not in any way to deter me from doing my duty to my Queen and Country as you will see."* He described the action he had seen since arriving in Cape Town on 12th November the previous year and… *"thank God our goal was reached - and captured - the capital of the Orange Free State."*

The Boer War: 1899-1902

Despite the successes, the war dragged on throughout 1901 with the vicar again recording the anxieties felt in the parish, *"about those serving in our armies in South Africa"*. It was finally brought to an end on May 31st 1902 with the signing of the Peace of Vereeniging.

What was learned from this colonial war only 12 years before 1914? One thing at least, as it resulted in British troops wearing khaki uniforms - a lesson the French army was not to learn until the First World War itself where their soldiers were easy targets for German machine guns in their bright blue uniforms.

Perhaps more should have been learned. Let us return to the United Patriots Supper of January 1900 where, amidst the patriotic fervour, some interesting truths were observed about the changing face of modern warfare. E. A. Wilson commented that: *"however valiant, however brave, however self-sacrificing they might be, they were no good against machine guns and unfortunately our soldiers went out with no other protection or little else than bravery and English pluck"*[7] - a sentiment echoed by the chairman, who remarked that: *"This war has awakened us (to the fact that)… in future we should not send our brave battalions out to be mown down by machine guns before they got a chance"*[8]

How spine-chillingly correct he was to be!

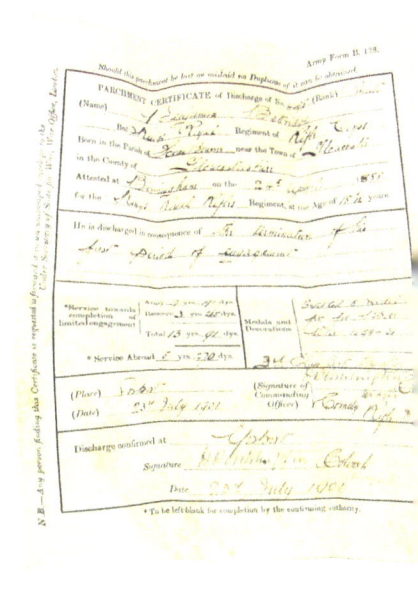

The discharge paper, gift tin from Queen Victoria (1900) and campaign medal for Private Benjamin Bettridge, Kings Royal Rifle Corps.
Courtesy of Hazel Mumford

7. *Evesham Journal, 6th January 1900*
8. *Ibid*

"We Will Remember Them"

LIGHTHORNE,
WARWICK.

Aug.13th,1914.

Dear Little,

It has been suggested that a Cavalry Squadron be formed among hunting men in Warwickshire, every man to find his own horse and equip himself when our services are called upon. Every man would be required to attend foot drills and mounted drills.

You would be free at any time to quit this force when offered another billet which might enable you "to go to the front" or obtain employment in any other capacity.

I propose to make the unit up to 120 strong and when the time comes we should offer ourselves as an additional squadron to the Warwickshire Yeomanry, join that Regiment and come under the command of Lt. Col. Frank Dugdale.

Any additions to the Squadron in the way of friends or employees would be acceptable.

I should be obliged if you would let me know as soon as possible if you are willing to join.

Yours sincerely,

Basil Hanbury.

Bidford and the First World War
Introduction

*'At the going down of the sun and in the morning,
we will remember them'*

These famous lines are spoken in many places throughout the world on or near the eleventh hour of the eleventh day of the eleventh month each year. In cities, towns and villages people young and old gather around war memorials to remember the dead and disabled of two world wars and many other conflicts since. As the years pass no one can now remember the men from this parish who gave their lives in the Great War of 1914-18. To many they are just a name we see on the war memorial or chancel screen in the church.

No one now remains alive who does remember them but should you choose to read the following pages, however, perhaps it will help to keep alive their memories for all time. Indeed, it will be a sad day should we ever forget the sacrifice these men made for us.

The summer of 1914 was very tense in Europe with many rumours of war in the air. The spark which was to light the powder keg happened with the assassination of the Archduke Franz Ferdinand in the Bosnian capital of Sarajevo on Sunday 28th June 1914. The war began on the 4th August taking in much of Europe, and by its end it would take in much of the world.

"We Will Remember Them"

"It will all be over by Christmas", they said. How wrong they were! Four years and nearly four months were to pass before peace was restored and men could return to 'a land fit for heroes'. In that time, nearly ten million were to die and over twenty one million would be wounded. The world would never be the same again. Very soon the names of Ypres, Mons, Arras, the Somme and Gallipoli would become known worldwide and sadly these places would take many Bidford lads, never to return them home.

Such horrors still seemed far away in August 1914 and at a meeting at the White Lion hotel (now flats) the Bidford Drill and Rifle Association was formed.
A committee was elected as follows:
President: Dr Fosbroke
Vice President and Treasurer: A. E. Bailey,
Vice President, W. H. Longford.
The committee – G. Leeman, T. Oliver, B. Whitcomb, W. H. Cowper,
and the Reverend J. W. Evans.
The drill instructor was to be Sergeant Major Cheshire from Haselor. Mr T. Heath kindly offered the loan of a field at Staple Hill for use as a firing range. (Staple Hill is to be found on the Honeybourne Road.) Messrs Kendrick offered the use of the Assembly Rooms (now demolished and where the Bridge Restaurant now stands) as the headquarters and meeting place. It was decided to hold drills at 6.30pm on Wednesday evenings across the river on the cricket pitch.

So it was that Bidford prepared and went to war. Many volunteered for Kitchener's new army, men already with the colours or on the reserve hurrying back to join their regiments.

The war, which was to bring so much heartache and tragedy to this then small community, began in earnest on the 2nd November 1914. Less than three months after the war began, young Harold Nicholls aged just 19, but nevertheless a regular soldier for nearly three years, from Ivy Cottage, Marlcliff, died in Poperinghe, Belgium of wounds received in action. For Bidford, the tragedy had begun.

Picture Right: Warwickshire Yeomanry
Picture courtsey of Rodney Compton collection

Chapter 2

The Way They Were: Life in Bidford on the Eve of War

*It begs the question, why did they rush off to enlist?
Was it patriotism? Was it the spirit of adventure?
Was it the chance to travel and see other places in this country
and abroad or was it the chance to escape
the hard working life and conditions they were enduring in 1914?
Whatever the reasons, the subsequent experiences
of these enthusiastic volunteers were to change
the nation's attitude to war forever.*

"We Will Remember Them"

Evesham Journal, 5th September, 1914: "Sunday, 30th August: a large and enthusiastic meeting was held on the Bank addressed by Colonel Ludlow of Birmingham. About 500 men were present." (Photograph courtesy of the Rodney Crompton Collection)

Before beginning the individual stories of the men of Bidford, it is only right to pause and look at life as it was in 1914. As an insight to this, where possible the census of 1911 has been used. From this, it is noticeable how people moved around in the early part of the twentieth century seeking employment. Though their names are on the village war memorial, quite a few were either not born in Bidford but their family lived in the village or they were born here but moved away to seek further employment.

The occupations varied from bricklayer to baker, miller to needle scourer, railway clerk to postman. The vast majority, however, were shown as farm labourers. Sadly, in 1911, some of them such as Ernest Ash and Gerald Gould were shown as schoolboys. In Gerald's case, he was only ten years old in 1911. He was destined to be the last Bidford man to die on active service on 8th November 1918 aged just eighteen.

The places where they moved to or from or indeed were born, are in themselves quite

The Way They Were: Life in Bidford on the Eve of War

interesting. Two of them had travelled as far as Canada seeking employment, others to the industrial towns of Redditch and Birmingham. Take, for instance, George Lane in 1911, living and working as an under-cowman at Fulwell, Enstone, in Oxfordshire. At the time he was living with his parents but had in fact been born in Chaddington, also in Oxfordshire. By the time of his death the family had moved again and were living and working in Broom.

Harry Wheatley, the postman, was born in Broadheath, Worcester, Charles Heaver in Godstone in Surrey, Louis Stanford at Buckland in Gloucestershire - and so it goes on. Apart from the two who emigrated, however, others born in the parish also moved away. Samuel Churchley, a bricklayer, had moved with his wife and young family to Evesham. Likewise, Edgar Harris, a groom and domestic gardener, was to be found living with his family at Owlet's End in Bengeworth, Evesham. Albert Collett, who in 1911 was living at 3 Coronation Row, Ickneild Street, was by the time of his death living at 122 Golden Hillock Road in Smallheath, Birmingham.

In reality, circumstances were not much different from today. People needed to be where the work was located and in the case of Bidford people, for the men it would have been the railway, Broom Mill, the Co-op or the bigger farms such as Broom Court or Blackwell's at Bickmarsh Hall.

Several were regular soldiers and perhaps in the case of Fred Tarrant he had enlisted to make life easier for his mother. Fanny Tarrant was a widow and in 1911 she was living in Salford Road with her son-in-law Martin Corton who was from Kiltinagh, County Mayo. His wife Louisa and younger sister Elsie were also in residence. To help with the finances, Fanny was working as a glove maker. So from this small insight, we can see that life in Bidford prior to the war was not easy. Long hours, low pay and rented or tied cottages.

An old soldier from that period, Bill Russell, who had been a Kitchener's Volunteer, said when he was interviewed, "we were working in the fields when war began. Some of us stopped what we were doing and went off to enlist." He said that they thought 'it would all be over by Christmas'. He went on to say that some had never even been out of the parish.

"We Will Remember Them"

Soldiers on horseback by Bidford Bridge
Photograph: Rodney Crompton Collection

It begs the question, why did they rush off to enlist? Was it patriotism? Was it the spirit of adventure? Was it the chance to travel and see other places in this country and abroad or was it the chance to escape the hard working life and conditions they were enduring in 1914? Whatever the reasons, the subsequent experiences of these enthusiastic volunteers were to change the nation's attitude to war forever.

"Cry 'havoc!' and let slip the dogs of war"
William Shakespeare: 'Julius Caesar': Act III, Sc. 1

Chapter 3

The Soldiers' Stories
1914

"we were working in the fields when war began. Some of us stopped what we were doing and went off to enlist. … we thought it would all be over by Christmas".
Bill Russell, a Kitchener's Volunteer

"We Will Remember Them"

Harold Arthur Nichols
Private 12878, second battalion.
Worcestershire Regiment.
Died: Monday 2nd November 1914
aged 19.
Buried in Poperinghe Old Military Cemetery,
Belgium (plot 1, grave 54)
Medals: 1914 Mons Star,
British and Victory medals.

Harold Nichols was the third son of Frederick and Fanny Nichols (nee Smith) of Ivy Cottage Marlcliff. His father was a house painter and the 1911 census shows Harold as a farm labourer. He had four brothers and two sisters.

Shortly after the 1911 census Harold left home and joined the army. He enlisted in Worcester, joining the Worcester 2nd Battalion at the age of 16. When war broke out he was stationed with his regiment at Aldershot and they sailed to France with the First British Expeditionary Force (known as the BEF) in August 1914. They then moved into Belgium to try and stem the German advance at Mons. Failing to do this, they took part in the heroic retreat from Mons, before standing and holding their ground outside the famous town of Ypres.

The Soldiers' Stories - 1914

At the beginning of 1915, his parents received news to say that their son had died of wounds received in action. These wounds had been received during the fighting between Zillebeke and Hooge. This would have been at Gheluvelt which was a famous action of World War I for the Worcesters. It was here that the German advance was finally halted.

On being wounded, Harold was taken to Number 5 casualty clearing station at Poperinghe in Belgium and it was here that he succumbed to his wounds. At the time of his death he had an elder brother in the army who had also been wounded, two brothers-in-law were also in the army. His grave is in a small walled-off area in the cemetery and is one of the earliest graves there. It is a very pretty, peaceful place.

Poperinghe Old Military Cemetery, Belgium

Site of the Christmas Truce football match, 1914

"We Will Remember Them"

The Soldiers' Stories - 1915

The first five months of the war were over and it was not, as they had been led to believe, over by Christmas. The old regular army of Britain had virtually ceased to exist by the end of 1914, Kitchener's Volunteers were not yet ready to be thrust into the fray and it was left to the remaining regulars and the Territorial Army to plug the gap. Many famous battles had been fought in this period – Mons, the Marne, Le Catauea and the first Ypres battle.

A million men were to die in those first five months and Bidford was fortunate to have lost only one. 1915 would see many more famous actions such as the Battles of Neuve Chappelle, Aubers Ridge, the second Battle of Ypres, Gallipoli and Loos. In 1915 Bidford would suffer its second highest fatalities of the war when 16 men were to lose their lives.

"Fierce fiery warriors fight upon the clouds
In ranks and squadrons and right form of war"
(William Shakespeare: 'Julius Caesar', Act II, Sc. 2)

Destruction during the Battle of Neuve Chappelle, 1915. (Photo IWM Q 51749)

"We Will Remember Them"

Harry Wheatley

**Private, 3rd Battalion,
Worcestershire Regiment.
Died: February 1915 aged 30.
Buried in unmarked grave
in Bidford churchyard.
Medals: British and Victory medals.**

Harry Wheatley (Henry John) was born at Broadheath, Worcester. The 1911 census shows him living in Bidford High Street with his wife Minnie and family. One of their children, Jack, was to be killed in Malta during the Second World War.

Harry had been in the army at the turn of the century obviously serving as a young lad and had been with the regiment in South Africa. On leaving the army in 1907 he was placed on the reserve list. In civilian life he gained employment with the Post Office as a postman in Bidford.

When war broke out, being a reservist, he was called up straight away. He successfully completed his training but, because of ill health, he was not sent overseas with his battalion. He was invalided out of the army in December 1914 and returned home to Bidford. Subsequently he died of ill health in early February 1915.

At his funeral on Thursday 11th February 1915, his bearer party was made up of men home on leave. A guard of honour included the postmaster and other postal workers with whom he had worked for the past seven years.

Thomas Arthur Richardson

Private, 6928, 3rd Battalion,
Worcestershire Regiment.
Died: Friday 12th March 1915 aged 29.
Commemorated on the Menin Gate Memorial,
Ypres, Belgium (panel 34).
Medals: 1914 Mons Star, British and Victory medals.

Thomas Richardson was born at Oversley, Alcester. Nothing is known of his early years except that he moved to Salford Priors with his parents. He became a regular soldier at the turn of the century, enlisted in Worcester and saw active service in South Africa during the Boer War. He left the army in 1907 and was placed on the reserve list.

He married his wife Olive, a Salford girl, in 1909 and, following this, they moved to live in Broom. The 1911 census shows them with one young daughter, Elizabeth, who was under the age of one. By the time of his death they had two more children. During this period he was employed as an agricultural labourer.

At the outbreak of war Thomas was called up by the regiment on 4th August 1914. Following training, he was sent to the Western Front. By March 1915 the battalion was in the Ypres Salient. They were located in reserve positions in the village of Kemmel. On the evening of the 11th March, the battalion was ordered up to the front line. They were to attack German positions around Spanbrockmolen. It was during this attack that Thomas was killed at Lemurhoch. His body was never recovered. At the time of his death his brother was recovering from wounds in a French hospital.

"We Will Remember Them"

Edwin Sheasby

**Gunner, 662, 109th Heavy Battery,
Royal Garrison Artillery.
Died: Monday 29th March 1915, aged 29.
Buried at St Sever Cemetery, Rouen,
France (plot A, row 6, grave 20).
Medals: 1914 Mons Star, British and Victory medals.**

Edwin Sheasby was the elder son of Arthur and Harriet Sheasby. He was born at Stoke, near Coventry in 1885. Shortly after he was born the family moved to Icknield Street in Bidford and Edwin was christened at St Laurence's church in September of that year. His brother William was born in Bidford.

Edwin became a regular soldier, enlisting in 1902 at the age of 17 at Gosport in Hampshire. He spent a total of 12 years with the Royal Garrison Artillery regiment, nine with the colours and three years on the reserve. During his army life he spent five years in India, seeing action on the northwest frontier, two years in Malta and the remaining time in England. On leaving the army he went to work with his father who was a builder by trade. This is shown in the 1911 census.

At the outbreak of war Edwin was called back to his old battery, the 109th. He was posted with them over to France at the end of 1914. During March 1915 he caught pneumonia and was sent to hospital in Rouen. It was here that he died on 29th March.

George Henry Fosbroke Power

Lieutenant, 3rd Regular Battalion,
Middlesex Regiment.
Died: Sunday 9th May 1915, aged 21.
Commemorated on the Menin Gate Memorial,
Ypres, Belgium (panels 49 & 51).
Medals: 1914-15 Star,
British and Victory medals.

George Henry Fosbroke Power was born on 7th January 1894 at 26 Bloomsbury Square London. He was the son of Sir D'Arcy Power KBE FRCS and Lady Eleanor Power. His mother was the daughter of Dr Fosbroke, the medical officer for Bidford. George was educated at the Merchant Tailors' Company School in London. On leaving school, he went for a short spell to train as a medical student at St Bartholomew's Hospital where his father was a surgeon. On leaving here, he went to New College Oxford and, being a keen sportsman, he soon became the President of the University Fencing Club. He also joined the university Officer's Training Corps in October 1912 where he held the rank of lance corporal. They were part of the 6th (reserve) battalion of the Middlesex Regiment.

On the outbreak of war, he applied for a full commission with a regular battalion on the 5th August 1914. He was given the rank of lieutenant and was posted to the 3rd battalion on their arrival back from garrison duty in Cawnpore, India. He sailed for France, landing at Le Havre as part of the 28th division on 19th January 1915. From here the battalion moved to the

"We Will Remember Them"

Ypres Salient. On the 8th/9th May 1915 the battalion took part in a famous attack on the Frezenberg Ridge near Ypres. It gained great praise for this action but at a terrible cost of seven officers and 338 other ranks. It was during this action, while attached to C Company, that George was reported missing on 8th May 1915.

Following this, his father wrote many times to the War Office asking for news of his son and it was not until 1919 that his death was finally confirmed. During this period many false trails appeared, indicating that he was still alive. One of these was that he was a prisoner-of-war. This was to involve lengthy correspondence with the Red Cross in Switzerland before it was found to be untrue. The family also issued a postcard with his picture on in the hope that he would be recognised.

Later on, the family solicitors received two statements from soldiers who had been with him at the time. One from Sergeant Garvey states that George was wounded in daylight on 9th May during terrible shellfire. Garvey was one of only 14 left in the company. The other report was from Private Worcester of A Company who stated that George had had his hand blown off but when they went back to look for him they could not find him.

His father finally received intelligence from Germany that his son had died on 9th May 1915 during the second Battle of Ypres at a German dressing station. He had been brought in unconscious with a severe shell wound to the right side and was buried the same day in the front garden of the Villa Tiegelei at Zonebeke. His estate could now be settled and everything was left to his brother. This included money as well as stocks and shares. His brother was also to receive his medals. His grave was never found again due to all the heavy shelling that took place in the area.

Menin Gate Memorial,
Ypres, Belgium (panels 49 & 51)

The Soldiers' Stories - 1915

Frederick Tarrant
**Private, 11625 4th Battalion,
Worcestershire Regiment.
Died: Friday 4th June 1915 aged 31.
Commemorated on the Helles Memorial,
Gallipoli (panels 104-113).
Medals: 1914-15 Star,
British and Victory medals.**

PTE. FREDERICK TARRANT, of the 4th Worcesters, son of Mrs. William Tarrant, of Bidford-on-Avon, who has been killed in action in the Dardanelles. Particulars are given in our Local War Notes on Page 12.

Fred Tarrant was the son of Fanny and the late William Tarrant and was born in Bidford. In 1911, his mother, who worked at glove-making, was living with her daughter Louisa and son-in-law, Martin Corton in Salford Road. Also living with them was Fred's other sister, Elsie.

Fred was a single man and serving as a regular soldier when war broke out. He had joined the army in January 1909, enlisting in Stratford-upon-Avon. Prior to this he had worked as an under-carter on a farm. In 1911 following training, he was posted with the 4th battalion of the Worcestershire Regiment to India. While there, he saw active service on the northwest frontier.

Following the outbreak of war, the battalion returned to England on 1st February 1915. They travelled by train to the Banbury area where they were billeted. They then moved to Warwick and were placed in billets around Leamington Spa. They left Leamington on 22nd March and travelled to Avonmouth from where the battalion sailed to Malta aboard four ships, the SS Southland, Caledonia, Aragon and Melville. They arrived in Malta on 31st March. From here they went to Alexandria by 4th April and then on to Lemnos, Cyprus by the 15th. They then headed for Cape Helles, Gallipoli where they landed on W Beach on 25th April 1915. Following two unsuccessful attacks on Krithia and Achi Baba, the British launched the third battle on 4th June 1915 and this is often referred to by its date as the Battle of the 4th of June.

It was during this attack, which the Worcesters began at noon, that Fred was killed; his body was never recovered. The battalion captured three lines of Turkish trenches that day but at a great cost.

By the time of Fred's death his mother had moved and was living in a cottage on the Salford Road.

As a point of interest, just over three weeks after Fred's death, 2nd Lieutenant Herbert James of Fred's battalion won the Victoria Cross. This was the regiment's first VC of the war. On the 6th August 1915 during the Battle of the Vineyard, the battalion Fred had known was almost completely destroyed.

Helles Memorial, Gallipoli

The Soldiers' Stories - 1915

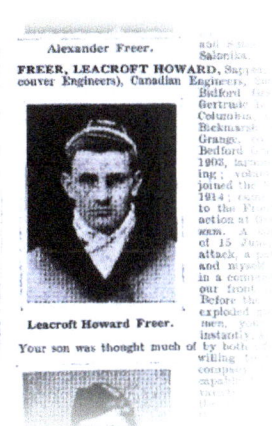

Leacroft Howard Freer

Sapper, 5089, 1st Field Company,
Canadian Engineers (6th North Vancouver).
Died: Tuesday 15th June 1915 aged 30.
Commemorated on the Vimy Ridge Memorial
(names in alphabetical order).
Medals: 1914-15 Star, British and Victory medals.

Leacroft Freer was born on 26th August 1884. He was the son of a farmer, Howard Freer and his wife, Gertrude Louisa (nee Davis). The family lived at Grange Farm, Bidford. It appears they were quite well off as they employed a governess, a cook and a housemaid. Following his father's death in 1892, the family moved to 11 Devon Road, Bedford, where Leacroft attended the local grammar school. In 1903 they emigrated to Canada and settled in Port Hammond, British Colombia. Leacroft, who never married, became a carpenter by trade.

At the outbreak of war he went with the first draft from North Vancouver on 26th August 1914. This was the 6th Field Company and they travelled by the Canadian Pacific Railway to Valcartier in Quebec. It was here that he was enrolled on 24th September 1914. Prior to the war he had been in the active militia. His attestation papers show him as 5' 8" tall, with grey eyes, fair hair and of good physical development.

Leacroft then sailed to England with the First Canadian Expeditionary Force. They arrived at Salisbury Plain on 20th October 1914 for further training.

On completion of training he was sent with the first field company of the First Canadian Expeditionary Force to France where they landed in February 1915. He was killed in action on 15th June at Givenchy. A comrade wrote to his mother the following: "On the evening of 15th June, the Canadians were making an attack. A party of engineers including your son and myself were waiting with some infantry in a communication trench immediately behind our front line for the word to go forward. Before the word came, a large German shell exploded quite close to us, killing seven of our men, your son being one. He was killed instantly as he was nearest to the explosion. Your son was thought much of by both officers and men. He was always so willing to help others. His services to the company will be greatly missed. He was so capable, being able to turn his hand to such a variety of works."

Then another wrote: "… *he was the ideal type of an Englishman. I always thought, and I know that everyone who had anything to do with him liked and admired him*".

*Leacroft Howard Freer
Regimental Record Sheet*

(Above) Leacroft Howard Freer Attestation Paper

The Soldiers' Stories - 1915

Edgar Harris

Private, 13729, D Company,
1st Battalion the Lincolnshire Regiment.
Died: Wednesday 16th June 1915 aged 30.
Commemorated on the Menin Gate Memorial, Ypres, Belgium (panel 21).
Medals: 1914-15 Star, British and Victory medals.

Edgar Harris was born in Littleton, the son of Major and Anne Harris. The 1911 census shows him living with his wife Annie Elizabeth (nee Lampitt) and two daughters, Edith and Irene, at Howletts End in Bengeworth, Evesham. At this time he was working as a groom and domestic/gardener. By the time of his death, the family were living in Barton and now had four children.

Edgar was an early volunteer, enlisting in Stratford-upon-Avon. After completing training, he was posted with the 1st battalion of the Lincolnshire Regiment to France in early 1915. By June the Lincolns were in positions in the Ypres Salient.

The next news of Edgar was when his wife received a telegram from the War Office dated 27th July 1915 informing her that Edgar was missing in action. She then received a letter from Edgar's company sergeant major informing her that Edgar had taken part in an attack on German positions on 16th June and had not been seen since. She must therefore assume that he had been killed in action. By coincidence, another Bidford man died on this day - Harry Freeman - with the Worcesters at Belewarde Lake, Belgium. Edgar's body was never recovered.

Following Edgar's death, his wife Annie later re-married, becoming Mrs Houghton.

"We Will Remember Them"

William Henry Freeman

Sergeant, 13202, 3rd Battalion, Worcestershire Regiment.
Died: Wednesday 16th June 1915 aged 32.
Commemorated on the Menin Gate Memorial, Ypres, Belgium (panel 34).
Medals: 1914 Mons Star, British and Victory medals.

Harry Freeman as he was known, was one of 6 children and the son of Justice and Mary-Ann Freeman (nee Plummer). The family lived in what was known as the Blocks in Salford Road, Bidford.

On leaving school, Harry enlisted in the army. He served as a regular soldier in the Royal Artillery and in 1901 was stationed at Crondall, Hampshire. On completion of his time he left the army and was placed on reserve. He joined the police force and was stationed at Sutton Coldfield.

The following story was told by a late relative of Harry who came from Birmingham. One night while on duty at the outbreak of war, Harry stopped a man for riding a cycle with no lights. On discovering that the man was an ex-army pal, he decided to let him go on the condition that he walked. When out of sight, however, the man re-mounted before being stopped again by Harry's sergeant. He told the sergeant how Harry had let him go and on returning to the station, Harry was informed that he was to be disciplined. He returned to Bidford the following day and here, outside the Bull's Head pub, Harry found the girl he was engaged to with another man. Harry was so furious that he snatched the engagement ring from her and threw it into the road.

This, and the thought of the disciplinary action, is probably what led him to go straight to Worcester and enlist with the regiment. As a reservist he went with the battalion to France on 12th August 1914 and took part in the early battles.

The Soldiers' Stories - 1915

An inscription commemorating Henry Freeman on the Menin Gate photo courtesy of Mick McCann of the British War Graves Commission

He was promoted to the rank of sergeant and moved with the battalion to the Ypres Salient in Belgium. The battalion was moved to positions near Bellewarde Lake. Harry had not been there long when one night a shell landed in the trench amongst him and his platoon. He was blown to pieces, dying instantly.

From the day of his enlistment to the time of his death he had not been home on leave. Due to the manner of his death no body was ever found. He was killed on the same day as another Bidford lad, Edgar Harris.

"We Will Remember Them"

The Soldiers' Stories - 1915

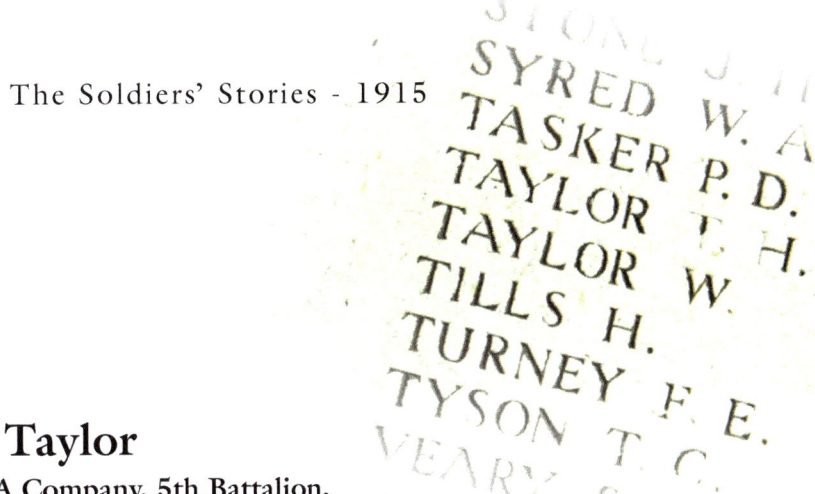

Thomas Henry Taylor

Lance Corporal, 12808, A Company, 5th Battalion,
Oxford & Bucks Light Infantry.
Died: Sunday 20th June 1915, aged 22.
Commemorated on the Ypres Menin Gate Memorial, Belgium (panels 37 & 39).
Medals: 1914-15 Star, British and Victory medals.

Thomas Taylor was the son of Joseph and Jane (nee Lane) Taylor and the family home was in the village of Barton where the father was employed as cart driver on a local farm. Thomas had three other brothers and two sisters. He himself worked as a farm labourer.

Thomas was an early volunteer and along with his brother Walter and friend William Bott, enlisted on 2nd September 1914. All three of them joined the Oxford & Bucks Light Infantry in Birmingham. Thomas was soon promoted to the rank of Lance Corporal and on completion of his training was posted with his friend to France in May 1915.

Soon after arriving in France the battalion was moved up to take part in the fighting around Ypres. It was during this time that Thomas was killed in action on 20th June 1915; his body was never found. He had died less than five weeks after his arrival at the front. His family were notified of his death in a letter home by his friend Private Bott.

This had been a bad time for Bidford, losing 4 of her men in just 6 days.

Pictured left, Lance Corporal Thomas Henry Taylor and pictured right with his brother, Walter Taylor (on left) (see page 98)
Courtesy of Doreen Bird and Nan Wesson

"We Will Remember Them"

Albert Edward Harris

Private, 9919,
1st Battalion, Royal Warwickshire Regiment.
Died: Saturday 31st July 1915, aged 30.
Buried at Sucrerie Military Cemetery,
Colincamps, France (plot 3, row A, grave 6).
Medals: 1914-15 Star,
British and Victory medals.

Albert Harris was born in Bidford. In 1901 he was aged 14 and working as an undercarter at Upper Lodge Farm, Oversley. Following his marriage, he moved to Binton with his wife Emma (nee Tysoe) and daughter Ellen-May. Before joining up, he was employed on the farm of Mr Charles Hodges of Binton working as a cowman. He had been working for Mr Hodges for five years and the farmer promised to keep his position open for him until the end of the war.

Albert enlisted in Stratford-upon-Avon in December 1914, joining the 3rd Battalion the Warwicks. His training began at the depot in Warwick before being completed at Parkhurst Camp, Newport, Isle of Wight. From here he was drafted to the 1st Warwicks and sent over to France. In June 1915 he received a wound to the shoulder but soon recovered from this. By July 1915 Albert's battalion was in position in the Somme region of France. The exact way he died is unknown - however, his wife received a letter dated 31st July from Albert's captain. He stated

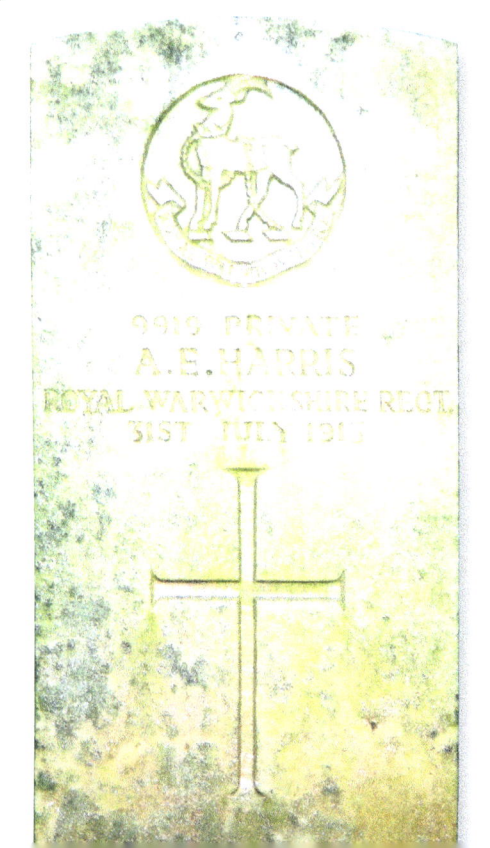

The Soldiers' Stories - 1915

how sorry he was to have to break the news of her husband's death and spoke highly of his character and example. He went on to say that Albert was cool and brave under fire and was well liked by all who knew him. It was, he said, the highest tribute he could pay any soldier. She then received a further letter from his friends in the company. They said that his death had been instantaneous and that in losing him they had all lost a friend.

At the time of his death, Albert had another brother in the army who had been previously wounded and spent seven weeks in hospital. By the time of Albert's death, he was fully recovered and was in camp at Wareham.

The Memorial Plaque (popularly known as the "Dead Man's Penny") was issued after the First World War to the next-of-kin of all British and Empire service personnel who were killed as a result of the war

Frederick Henry Wright

Private 23038, Y Company, 4th Battalion.
Worcestershire Regiment.
Died: Friday 6th August 1915, aged 19.
Commemorated on the Helles Memorial,
Gallipoli (panels 104-113).
Medals: 1914-15 Star,
British and Victory medals.

PTE. FREDERICK WRIGHT (missing)..

Fred Wright was the son of Frederick and Alice Wright (nee Hall) of New Cottages, Barton. Fred himself was born at Harescombe in Gloucestershire. Before the war he worked as a farm labourer.

Fred enlisted in the army in 1914, joining up in Birmingham. He joined the Worcestershire Regiment and on completion of training he was drafted into Y Company, the 4th Battalion. This battalion was part of the 29th Division. In March 1915 Fred was in billets in Leamington Spa. On 22nd March they embarked for Malta, sailing from Avonmouth. They arrived on the 31st and the following day sailed for Lemnos and then on to Mudros in Greece. Fred sailed for Gallipoli on 24th April 1915. Y Company landed on W Beach on the 25th and with three other companies advanced up Hill 138, attacking an enemy redoubt. He then took part in the advance on Krithia on the 27th to 28th April. On 1st May he was involved in an attack to regain lost ground following a Turkish attack. He was in action again on 6th May when the battalion gained a ridge 500 yards in front of the firing line.

He moved into rest camp on 11th May but even here they could still be shelled or sniped at by the Turks. On 16th May they moved back into the reserve line and on the 23rd were in the firing line between Twelve Tree Copse and Gully Ravine. Fred spent

The Soldiers' Stories - 1915

most of June in and out of the front line. He again saw action at Gully Ravine on 2nd July. On 15th July he withdrew to Gully Beach and on the 17th sailed for Lemnos aboard the Swiftsure. A party was held on board on the 25th attended by fewer than 200 men including seven officers. This was all that remained from a strength of 26 officers and 930 other ranks who had landed in April.

The battalion landed back on W Beach on 28th July. On Friday 6th August 1915 Fred took part in his final action. The company attacked the Vineyard, attacking trench H13 at 3.50pm. The leading waves were cut down crossing the 300 yards of no-man's land by machine gun fire from the front and both flanks. Sadly, Fred was one of those who was killed. On this day in August the battalion ceased to exist as he would have known it – it was wiped out.

"We Will Remember Them"

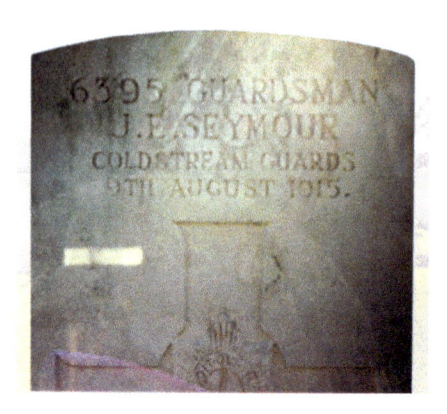

John Ernest Seymour

Private 6395,
3rd Battalion, Coldstream Guards.
Died: Monday 9th August 1915, aged 27.
Buried at Lillers Communal Cemetery, France
(plot 4, row A, grave 12).
Medals: Mons Star,
British and Victory medals.

John Seymour was the son of John and Minnie Seymour (nee Russell) and had been born in Bidford. He had been a regular soldier, joining the army in 1905 in Stratford-upon-Avon, serving with the Coldstream Guards. He did seven years with the regiment before being placed on the reserve in 1912. On leaving the army, he lived on the Salford Road in Bidford with his wife Maud (nee Gould) and son Ernest. His occupation between leaving the army and the outbreak of war is unknown.

He was recalled to the colours on 5th August, the day after war was declared. He reported to the barracks at Chelsea and sailed with the regiment as part of the 4th (Guards) Brigade, 2nd Division. They landed at Le Havre on 13th August 1914. John saw much action in the early days, taking part

42

The Soldiers' Stories - 1915

in the Battle of Mons and the subsequent retreat to the Marne. He then came home for a time, suffering from the effects of rheumatism. None of this, however, would have taken place with the 3rd Grenadiers as they had been stationed at Wellington Barracks from August 1914 until 26th July 1915. One must assume that John was drafted to the 3rd battalion following his period of illness. They sailed from Southampton aboard the Queen Alexandra, a Clyde steam boat, on the evening of the 26th, landing at Le Havre on 27th July. The 28th found them at St Omer and on the 29th at Esquedres. The 1st August, a Sunday, was church parade and on 2nd August they were at Helfout for company training. On 5th August the officers and sergeants went by motor bus to St Venant to view trench mortars in action. There is a gap in the battalion diary from the 9th to the 12th August 1915. John died of wounds on 9th August and it is probable that he was hit while digging trenches on that day. He was taken to hospital in Lillers where his death was recorded.

CERTIFIED COPY OF ENTRY OF DEATH
SAW 038536
Application Number 5390237-1
Registration of Births, Deaths and Marriages (Special Provisions) Act 1957

Return of Warrant Officers, Non-Commissioned Officers and Men of the Coldstream Guards Killed in Action or who have died whilst on Service Abroad in the War of 1914 to 1921

Rgtl. or Army number	Rank	Name in Full (Surname First)	Age	Country of Birth	Date of Death	Place of Death	Cause of Death
6395	Private	SEYMOUR John Ernest	27	England	9th Aug. 1915	Lillers	Died of Wounds

An Entry relating to the death of John Ernest Seymour

CERTIFIED to be a true copy of the ~~certified copy of~~* an entry in a Service Departments Register. Given at the General Register office, under the seal of the said Office, the 28th day of January 2014

"We Will Remember Them"

Whitmore Clarke

Corporal, 11788, 2nd Battalion,
Hampshire Regiment.
Died: Friday 13th August 1915, aged 25 years.
Commemorated on the Helles Memorial, Gallipoli
(panels 125-134).
Medals: 1914-15 Star,
British and Victory medals.

Whitmore Clarke was born in 1890 in Sedgeley, Staffordshire. He was the son of William and Annie Jane Clarke (nee Lathbury). He had four brothers and four sisters. His father was a builder/foreman and 'Whit', as he was known locally, was a bricklayer. By 1914 the family was living in Salford Road, Bidford. Whitmore was a single man and living at the family home. He was very popular in local football circles and a keen member of the Bidford team.

Shortly after war broke out he travelled to Birmingham in September 1914. Here he enlisted in the Duke of Cornwall's Light Infantry. He was then transferred to the 2nd Hampshires and was soon promoted to corporal. In August 1915 he was on board the HMS Royal Edward as part of a replacement draft heading for Gallipoli. While sailing through the Aegean Sea, she was sighted by a Turkish submarine, UB14, which fired a torpedo hitting the Royal Edward and causing her to sink. One can only imagine the panic there was on board. Of over 1,600 men only about 600 were saved. Sadly, Whitmore was not one of them. Amongst those lost were 212 men of the Hampshire Regiment. Their destination had been Gully Beach at Gallipoli.

His parents were informed by the War Office that their son, a corporal in the 2nd Hampshire Regiment, 29th Field Force, Mediterranean Expeditionary Force, was

The Soldiers' Stories - 1915

missing feared drowned upon the sinking of his troop ship on Friday 13th August 1915. It must be assumed that Whitmore's body went down with the ship.

HMS Royal Edward
Those drowned were listed as -
2nd Hampshires 207 & 5 officers
1st Essex regiment 107
Royal Army Medical Corps 143
& 4 officers
RASC 119 & 2 officers,
1st Border Regiment 59
2nd South Wales Borderers 53
1st King's Own Scottish Borderers 48
1st Lancashire. Fusiliers 27
& 1 officer
(Temp. Major Cuthbert Bromley, V.C.),
Royal Engineers 1

Arthur Rose

Lance Corporal, Y/1225, 2nd Battalion, King's Royal Rifle Corps.
Died: Friday 1st October 1915, aged 21.
Buried in Choques Military Cemetery, France (plot 1, row E, grave 105).
Medals: 1914-15 Star, British and Victory medals.

Lance.-Corp. A. ROSE (killed).

Arthur Rose was the son of Henry James and Sarah Ann Rose (nee Churchley) and the family lived in Salford Road, Bidford. Arthur had four brothers and one sister. The census of 1911 shows him employed as a market gardener's labourer.

When war broke out Arthur was an early volunteer, enlisting in Birmingham on 28th August 1914. On completion of training he was posted to France with the 2nd Battalion the King's Royal Rifle Corps in January 1915. He was wounded in action on May 9th, receiving a wound to the arm. This was, however, not serious and he was fit enough to return to the front in

July 1915. By September the battalion was in a rest area near the town of Bethune. On September 25th 1915 they moved up to the front to take part in an attack on German positions. Following this attack, Arthur was reported as missing. Two days later several volunteers went out to search for any survivors who might have been missed by the stretcher bearers. They found Arthur lying in no-man's land. He had been wounded through the right thigh. He was exhausted but they managed to bring him round and on seeing familiar faces he seemed to brighten up. He was placed on a stretcher, made comfortable and taken to a dressing station. From here he was sent down the line to Number 1 Casualty Clearing Station at Choques. Sadly, he did not recover from his wounds and died 4 days later on 1st October 1915.

His family did not receive news of his death until 22nd October. As in many cases, the cemetery where he is buried grew from the many who died from their wounds while being treated at the nearby Casualty Clearing Station.

"We Will Remember Them"

Thomas Albert Russell
Private, 11765,
2nd Battalion, Oxford & Bucks Light Infantry.
Died: Monday 4th October 1915, aged 20.
Buried in Boulogne Eastern Cemetery, France
(plot 8, row C, grave 44).
Medals: 1914-15 Star,
British and Victory medals.

PTE. T. A. RUSSELL
(killed).

Thomas Russell was the son of Henry and Julia Russell (nee Davies) of Tower Hill, Bidford. The census of 1911 shows the family living at the Grange, Bidford. His father was a farm carter and Thomas was shown as employed by 'seaming'. He had four sisters and two brothers.

He was an early volunteer, enlisting in Birmingham in September 1914. Following training, he was posted to France in early 1915 with the 2nd Battalion the Oxford and Bucks Light Infantry and he wrote his last letter home on 29th August 1915 in which he stated that he was "quite well" but had had "a few narrow squeaks". He had lost a chum who had been "knocked over by a bomb" whilst standing at his side. He went on to thank his mother for the parcel he had received and he bet they did not realise that it would end up only twelve yards from "old Fritz" before reaching her "poor Tommy"! (The lines were so close together.)

September found Thomas and his battalion as part of the 2nd Division at the Battle of

48

The Soldiers' Stories - 1915

Loos. The offensive began on 25th September under the direct orders of Lord Kitchener who said, "We must attack in order to do our utmost to help the French in their offensive, even though by doing so we may suffer heavy losses."

On the 21st September a diversionary attack took place north of La Bassee Canal at Givenchy which included the 2nd Oxford and Bucks. Thomas's battalion attacked at 6.am and they found the German front line trench empty. On attacking the second line, they came under heavy rifle and machine gun fire. Hand to hand fighting took place and it was noted how good the German hand grenades were. By 9.40am they were back in their own lines, having achieved nothing.

One must assume that this is where Thomas was wounded. Initially he would have been taken to a dressing station and then moved to a casualty clearing station and on by train to hospital in Boulogne. It was here that he died on Monday 4th October 1915. Normal fatalities in World War I were at a ratio of one in four, however at Loos it was one in two. As Kitchener said, they had indeed paid a heavy price.

Boulogne Eastern Cemetery, France (Picture: Wernervc)

"We Will Remember Them"

Private 10698 John Corbett Smith

B Company, 10th Battalion, Royal Warwickshire Regiment.
Died: Sunday 10th October 1915, aged 42.
Buried in Merville Communal Cemetery,
France (plot 4, Row H, grave 8).
Medals: 1914-15, British and Victory medals.

John Smith was the son of Sophia (nee Court) and the late Thomas Vardy Smith. He had two brothers, George and Oliver. He was a single man who lived with his mother on Tower Hill, Bidford. The census for 1911 shows him working as a farm labourer.
He joined up on 18th January 1915 in Stratford. Prior to this he had spent seven years with the county militia. He joined the 10th Warwicks and, as he was an excellent shot, trained as a battalion sniper. On completion of his training he was posted to France on 19th July 1915.

The next news of John was when his mother received a letter from the Sister in charge of the 2nd London Casualty Clearing Station in France. The letter stated that her son John had been admitted with dangerous head wounds and his condition was extremely serious. This was dated 9th October 1915. She received a telegram the following day to say that he had died of his wounds. However, the report in the battalion diary by his

50

company commander differs from this. He states that Private Smith had been shot in the head and had died in the ambulance en route to hospital, the fatal shot coming from a German sniper's rifle. It is very rare to see other ranks named in casualty reports in battalion diaries. John was one of three Bidford lads to die in the first ten days of October.

He was, however, the last of 1915.

"We Will Remember Them"

The Soldiers' Stories - 1916

The year of 1915 had been a bad year for Bidford, losing 16 of her men to the war. The year 1916 was to be noted for the terrible battle of the Somme which began on the 1st July and finally petered out in late November 1916. It was, however, the 1st July which was the date that would never be forgotten. Kitchener's Volunteers, including many of the Pals Battalions, went into action on this bloody day. Following a week long massive bombardment, the idea was that the army would advance at walking pace and occupy the German positions as no one would be left alive. This went terribly wrong as most of the German troops had sheltered in their bunkers deep underground. The attack was scheduled for 7.30am but the British blew a mine at 7.20. This alerted the Germans that the attack was about to begin. They came up from their bunkers, manning the firing bays with rifles and machine guns. As the British advanced, they opened fire and by the end of the day the British casualties were nearly 60,000, of whom just over 19,000 were killed. Most of these losses occurred in the first hour.

Prior to the battle, Bidford had only lost one of her men in 1916 - Gunner William Mumford – who died of wounds received in Belgium during the month of March. Surprisingly, no men from Bidford died on the first day of the Somme. Three more would die elsewhere but the Somme would eventually claim eight of the 1916 fallen from Bidford.

> *'The noise of battle hurtled through the air.*
> *Horses do neigh and dying men did groan'*
> (William Shakespeare: 'Julius Caesar' Act II, Sc. 2)

A German trench occupied by British Soldiers near the Albert-Bapaume road at Ovillers-la-Boisselle, July 1916 during the Battle of the Somme. (Photograph courtesy of Imperial War Museum - Q 3990)

William Thomas Mumford

Gunner, 64813, A Battery, 90th Brigade, Royal Field Artillery.
Died: 22nd March 1916 aged 27.
Buried at Lijssenhoek Military Cemetery, Belgium (plot 5, row D, grave 14).
Medals: 1914-15 Star, British and Victory medals.

William Mumford was the son of Thomas and Theresa Mumford (nee Sandals, later Teal) of 196 Long Street, Dorden, near Atherstone, Warwickshire. William was born in 1889 at Little Buckland, Gloucestershire. He married his wife, Florence Kate Smith in 1910. The census of 1911 shows him working as a farm carter living at Old Fallow, Little Comberton, Pershore. By the outbreak of war the family was living in Tower Hill, Bidford. William by then was working as a carter for Lane's at Broom Court Farm.

William enlisted in the army at Warwick in January 1915. He joined the Royal Field Artillery and on completion of his training arrived in France on 20th July 1915. At the beginning of 1916 the battery was in position in the Ypres Salient, Belgium.

The battery was in action on 21st March when William received severe wounds to the neck. He was taken to a casualty clearing station but died of these wounds the following day. He had been due to go home on leave shortly after, and the family had been greatly looking forward to his visit since he had not had any leave since arriving in France. In a letter to Florence, his battery major expressed his deepest sympathy and testified to his loyal devotion to duty. He left a widow and two small sons, Les and Jack.

*William Mumford,
his wife, Florence Kate
and their two sons Les and Jack.*

"We Will Remember Them"

William George Lane
Private, 22155,
1st Battalio, Worcestershire Regiment.
Died: Friday 7th July 1916 aged 20.
Buried at Mericourt-le-Abbe Communal Cemetery Extension, France (plot 2, row C, grave 17).
Medals: 1914-15 Star,
British and Victory medals.

William Lane was the son of Edwin and Bessie Lane (nee Townley) and was born in Chaddington, Oxfordshire. The census of 1911 shows the family living in Fulwell, also in Oxfordshire. His father Edwin was employed as a cowman and William as an under-cowman. Prior to the war the family had moved again, this time to Broom Court Lodge, Steppes Piece, Bidford.

William enlisted in the army on 18th April 1915 in Evesham. On completion of his training he was posted to France in March 1916. His regiment, the Worcesters, was one of those which was to be used on the Somme. Only four months after arriving in France, his parents received information that William had died as a result of wounds received in action. He received these wounds when the battalion attacked a German position known as Quadrangle Trench at the village of Contalmaison. This attack took place on the seventh day of the Battle of the Somme. Battalion records of the time showed his grave at

The Soldiers' Stories - 1916

map reference 62D NE 1/40000 square J4063. Two of his comrades were also buried at the same spot. Later, his body was exhumed and re-buried.

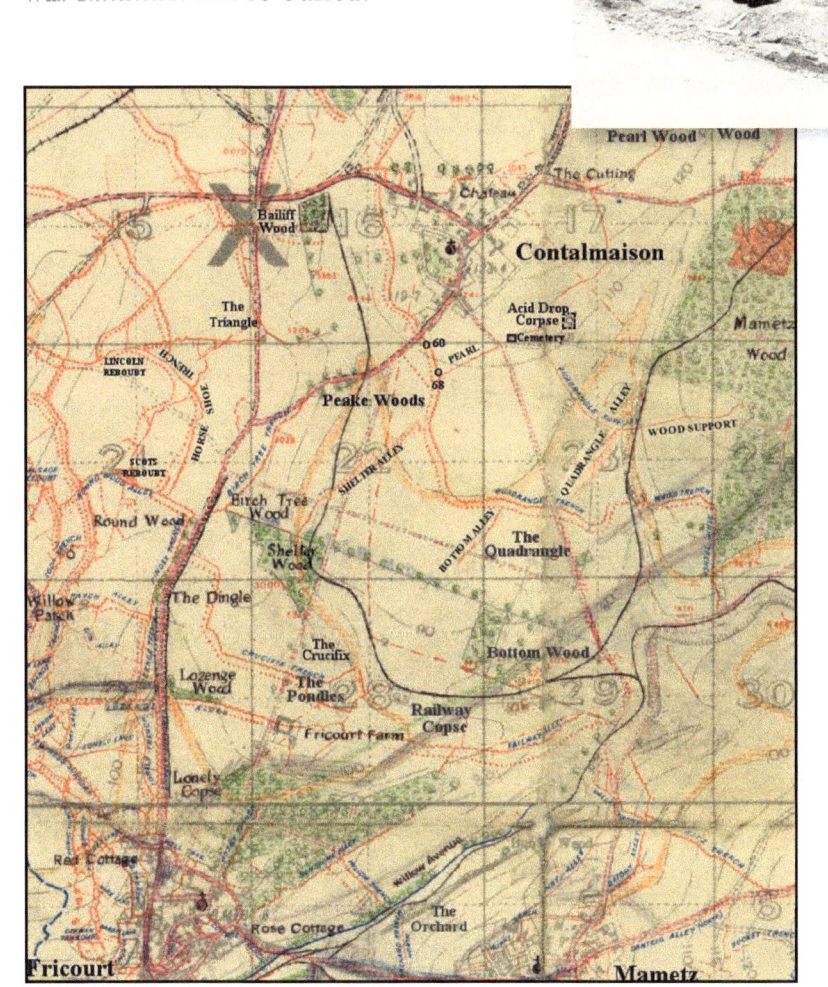

Sunken Road leading to Contalmaison July 1916 (Photo IWM Q859)

Map showing the German position known as Quadrangle Trench at the village of Contalmaison (Worcestershire Regiment Archieve)

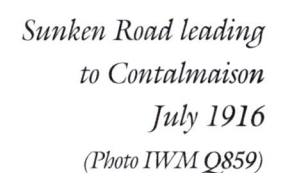

Herbert Leonard Davis
Private, 6897,
3rd Battalion, Worcestershire Regiment.
Died: Monday 10th July 1916, age 34.
Commemorated on the Thiepval Memorial,
France (pier 5a, panel 6c).
Medals: 1914-15 Star,
British and Victory medals.

Herbert Davis was born in 1882, the son of Emma Elizabeth Davis who was born in Inkberrow, Worcestershire in 1861. A year before Herbert was born, his mother had moved to Crabbs Cross where she was lodging with a family called Bayliss and was employed as a fishing tackle maker. In 1883 Emma married Walter Russell and they lived on Tower Hill, Bidford. They had four sons and a daughter and their youngest son Reginald, who was Herbert's step-brother, was killed in August 1914. By 1901 Herbert was working as a cowman at a farm in Abberton in Worcestershire. By 1911 he had moved a few miles to Kington where he worked as a wagoner at Red House Farm (pictured above). Living with him at the time was his own sister, Edith Morrall, a widow, and George Russell, one of his step-brothers.

Herbert enlisted in 1914 at Worcester. His enlistment papers had spelt his name as Davies which has not helped when researching him. The Memorial and all other documents are correct with the spelling shown as Davis. He joined the 3rd Battalion the Worcestershire Regiment, landing in France on 7th April 1915. The battalion took part in the Battle of Hooge in Belgium when the Germans used flame throwers for the first time. On 15th October 1915 the battalion became part of the 25th Division and

The Soldiers' Stories - 1916

took part in the second attack at Bellewarde. By May 1916 Herbert would have been in defensive positions, following German attacks at Vimy Ridge in France. The Battle of the Somme began on 1st July 1916 and on the 3rd Herbert would have taken part in the costly attack near the village of Thiepval. Following this attack, he moved up with his battalion on the evening of 9th July through the village of La Boiselle. The following day, 10th July, the Worcesters attacked the village of Ovillers and it was during this attack that Herbert was killed. The battalion lost three officers and six other ranks in the attack. One officer and three of other ranks were killed by enemy shellfire and, as Herbert's body was never found, he may well have been one of those killed by the shellfire.

Herbert Davis is amongst these soldiers from the 3rd Battalion the Worcestershire Regiment. Location unkown.
Photograph: Tony Bolton

59

"We Will Remember Them"

Pte. A. HARTLAND,
Oxon. & Bucks. L.I.
(Killed).

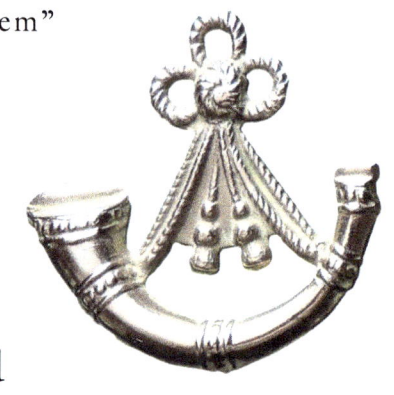

Arthur Hartland

Private, 11772, 2nd Battalion
Oxford and Bucks Light Infantry.
Died: Saturday 29th July 1916 aged 26.
Commemorated on the Thiepval Memorial, France (pier 10, faces A & D).
Medals: 1914-15 Star,
British and Victory medals.

Arthur Hartland was the son of Mr George William and Hannah Hartland. The 1911 census shows him living in Broom with his elder brother George and younger brother Sam, and his occupation is shown as a farm worker.

Following the outbreak of war, he travelled to Birmingham where he enlisted in the army on 1st September 1914 with the Oxford and Bucks Light Infantry. As his battalion had sailed to France at the end of August, he was sent down to Hampshire for his basic training. On completion of this he sailed to France with a reinforcement draft on 1st June 1915. By this time he had become a battalion signaller. He landed in France on 22nd June which was also his 25th birthday. In early 1916 the battalion was located first at Bethune and then Festubert. In June they received a new commanding officer, Lieutenant-Colonel Richard Crosse who was to be their commanding officer for the next three years.

On 23rd June 1916 the battalion moved from billets up to the front in preparation for the forthcoming Somme battle. On 28th July the battalion moved up to Waterlot Farm to relieve the 2nd Highland Light Infantry. The following day, while out collecting water with others, he was killed instantly by shell fire. His remains were buried in Bernafy Wood by his friends. A casualty clearing station was also located there.

The Soldiers' Stories - 1916

The first news that his family received of his death was in a letter sent to his brother Sam from a pal in France. Following the heavy fighting and shelling that took place in that area his grave was never found again.

Four days before his death, Arthur wrote this letter to his brother:

"I am quite well at the present, but the Lord only knows who will be left of us in a day or two's time. We are in a large camp which very much resembles those hills and valleys around Grafton and Fammington. There are thousands of us here, also the cavalry. I can't tell you where we are, but we are here for the big push where all the fighting has been going on since July 1st. We left billets on June 23rd. We are going up to-night, but when we go into action nobody knows, but I guess it will be in a day or two. The bombardment is just like hell itself, as the saying is. There are a lot coming down wounded, day and night. I saw a lot of German prisoners when we were on the way up here. Some of them looked very young, also small, but they seemed pleased to be taken prisoners. I wouldn't have missed the sight round here for anything. It seems all like one large machine, men, horses, motor transports by the thousand. If you could see it you would wonder where it all comes from. There's more coming off round here than we are aware of, but we are here to beat them this time or die. If you don't hear from me for a week or two try and keep mother and dad cheered up as much as you can. If I come through it all right I shall send you a p.c. as soon as I can, but if you don't hear from me don't be alarmed, because there's a chance of getting wounded and several things without getting killed. Of course, if it's my luck to go under you must all take it as well as possible, because whatever happens it's God's wish, but I have good faith in coming through all right. I hope we can push them right back when we are at it. There's no mistake our artillery is playing havoc with them. One can't describe what it's like unless they are here to witness it."[9]

Thiepval war memorial
Photograph courtesy of Mick McCann, British War Graves

9. Evesham Journal 1916

"We Will Remember Them"

Fred McQuay

Private, 215, 14th Battalion,
(1st City of Birmingham)
Royal Warwickshire Regiment.
Died: Sunday 30th July 1916 aged 26.
Commemorated on the Thiepval Memorial,
France (pier 9, A & B, pier 10, B).
Medals: 1914-15 Star, British and Victory medals.

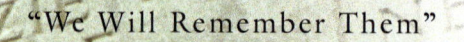

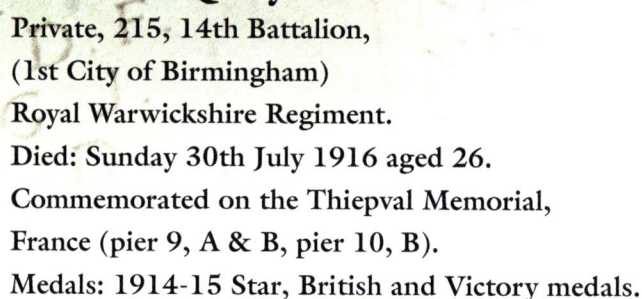

Fred McQuay was born in Redditch on 28th July 1890. He was the son of Frederick and Sarah Catherine (nee Clarkson) McQuay and also had a sister, Kate. His father was a draper and his mother a tailoress and they owned their own shop in Redditch. The 1911 census shows Fred living at 14 and 15 Market Place, Redditch. He was employed as a draper and warehouseman. Prior to the war he moved to London as a trainee shop manager at Marshall and Snellgrove. He was never to marry. His parents owned a cottage close to the River Arrow at Broom as his father was a keen fisherman. Fred also loved the water and kept his own canoe on the Avon at Bidford.

Fred was amongst the first 1,000 volunteers in August 1914 as his army number shows. He enlisted at the Birmingham Post newspaper offices in August 1914 and joined the 14th Battalion (1st city of Birmingham) Royal Warwickshire Regiment. Fred did his initial training at Sutton Park in Birmingham and Wensleydale in north Yorkshire. Here he became a member of the battalion's machine gun section and sailed to France on 21st November 1915.

The battalion became part of the 5th Division and in early 1916 was located at the

Photograph of Fred McQuay courtesy of Robert McCrorie

The Soldiers' Stories - 1916

Fred McQuay, firing machine gun. Photograph courtesy of Joan McCrorie

southern end of Vimy Ridge. Here they took part in trench raids, sniping and mining. On 1st July they were in GHQ reserve re-fitting and resting. On 28th July Fred celebrated his 26th birthday. On 29th July the battalion moved up to the village of Longueval. They were to attack German positions north west of the village. They attacked the area of Wood Lane in an attempt to capture the infamous High Wood. The battalion was repulsed and sustained 171 casualties. The following day, while Fred was manning his machine gun, he was shot in the head and killed by a German sniper. His parents placed an inscription in the Redditch Indicator on 26th August 1916. It simply said, "He answered the call". Fred's death is also inscribed on the base stone of the grave of his brother-in-law, Charles Holder, in Bidford churchyard.

"We Will Remember Them"

Edward George Dee

Corporal, Y/1227, 9th Battalion,
King's Royal Rifle Corps.
Died: Thursday 24th August 1916, aged 23.
Buried in Delville Wood cemetery, Longueval,
France (plot 3, row K, grave 6).
Medals: 1914-15 Star, British and Victory medals.

Edward Dee was the only son of Mr and Mrs Francis Dee (nee Salmon). He had been born in Stratford-upon-Avon and the family had lived in Ryon Hill. As a lad he had played the organ at Ingon. The family then moved to Barton as publicans, taking over the Cottage of Content. Edward was keen to be involved in Bidford parish life; he was a member of the choir and raised money to defray the cost of the choir outing. He also raised funds to help start a football team. In peacetime he was a popular young man in both Barton and Bidford.

At the outbreak of the war Edward was the first man from Barton to volunteer. He enlisted in Birmingham on 24th August 1914 and was posted to Sheerness in Kent for his basic training. He went overseas to France with his regiment, the King's Royal Rifle Corps, in August 1915 and was to celebrate his 23rd birthday in June 1916 just days before the Battle of the Somme began on 1st July. He was promoted to Corporal in the field and was soon recommended for promotion to sergeant. In his last letter home just six weeks prior to his death, he said he was in the midst of the fray. His parents were notified shortly after that he had been killed in action on 24th August 1916 near to Delville Wood. It was known to the troops as Devil's Wood and many thousands of bodies still lie beneath it.

HOME ON LEAVE.

HOME IS HOME in every sense of the word to this war-worn Tommy home on leave. In place of the general rush and discomfort of an ordinary wash-day, he finds a bright little wife doubly happy in the joy of his visit, and in the knowledge that by merely soaking her clothes in cold water and Rinso, the clothes have washed themselves and enabled her to devote all her time to her husband's comfort and well-being.

Cold water is the fighting man's cleanser at the front, and at home his wife enjoys extra leisure from the fact

George Leonard

Lieutenant Quartermaster, 8th Battalion, South Staffordshire Regiment.
Died: Friday 1st September 1916, aged 53.
Buried in Le Treport Military Cemetery, France (plot 2, row O, grave 10).
Medals: DCM Long Service medal, 1914-15 Star, British and Victory medals.

George Leonard was born in Birmingham, the son of Joseph and Harriet Leonard (nee Hawtrier). He had five sisters and two brothers. From there the family moved to Handsworth in Birmingham. The census of 1911 shows him living at 4 Millsbro Road, Redditch. At this time he is shown as an army pensioner and a works inspector.

On 11th April 1911 he married Minnie and they moved to Alcester Road in Bidford. They had three sons, George, Clifford and William.

George had been a regular soldier, enlisting in the 1st South Staffords on 30th April 1885 and serving until 29th April 1906, attaining the rank of Colour Sergeant. During the Boer War in 1900 he won the Distinguished Conduct Medal for gallantry. This is second only to the Victoria Cross.

The Soldiers' Stories - 1916

He re-enlisted on 7th August 1914 with the rank of private. He was posted the next day to the 8th Battalion with the rank of Quartermaster Sergeant.

He would have been responsible for the battalion's supplies, billeting etc. He was commissioned on 3rd March 1915 and sent over to France in June 1915 ahead of his battalion who arrived on 14th July 1915. In August 1916 he fell ill and was admitted into the large base hospital at Le Treport and diagnosed with Cholecystitus which is inflammation of the gall bladder. His wife received official notification in early September saying that he had died in hospital as a result of his illness. She then received a letter from the Privy Purse at Buckingham Palace which said that the King and Queen deeply regretted the loss to her and the army due to the death of her husband while in the service of his country. It concluded by saying that, "Their Majesties truly sympathise with you in your sorrow".

After George's death his wife and children moved to what is now the chemist's shop, High Street, Bidford-on-Avon, where they ran a small sweet shop with Mrs Leonard's mother. He left £157.2s in his will. Sadly, Minnie died in September 1921. Le Treport cemetery is located 30 kilometres north east of Dieppe.

Albert Collett

Private 16326, 14th Battalion,
(1st City of Birmingham)
Royal Warwickshire Regiment.
Died: Tuesday 5th September 1916, aged 22.
Buried at La Neuville British Cemetery, France
(plot 2, row B, grave 54).
Medals: 1914-15 Star, British and Victory medals.

Albert or 'Bert' Collett was the son of John and Ellen Collett (nee Thornton) of Tower Hill, Bidford. He had a brother, James, and three sisters, Elizabeth, Catherine and Hilda. The census of 1911 shows them living at 3 Coronation Row, Icknield Street and at this time Albert was employed as a farm labourer.

Albert was an early volunteer and enlisted in the King's Royal Rifle Corps at Stratford-upon-Avon on 26th September 1914. He was, however, discharged after only ten weeks as being medically unfit. He re-joined in February 1915, again at Stratford, and this time he joined the 1st Birmingham Pals. He was drafted to France in November 1915 on completion of his training.

Following periods at the Front he was sent home on leave in May 1916. On May 23rd he married Marie and they were to set up home at 122 Golden Hillock Road, Smallheath in Birmingham. Sadly, however, he had to join his regiment one day later on 24th May 1916. It was the last time Marie was to see him alive. He landed back in France just five weeks prior to his death. The Pals were involved in several actions on the Somme, being part of the 13th Brigade of the 5th Division. He would have been involved in attacks on Wood Lane on 22nd July and Longueval on 30th July. Like Thomas Mayrick, he was involved in the attack on Falfemont Farm on 3rd September 1916.

He sent his last letter home on that day stating he was well. The objective was the German strongpoint known as the gun pits located in the valley south west from Wedge Wood. The Pals received heavy casualties during the advance on the German second line and withdrew to Dublin Trench on the Maricourt to Montaubon Road. It was during this attack that Albert was wounded. Sadly, he was to die of these wounds just two days later. The attack cost the Pals 303 casualties and Albert became the second of Bidford's 1st Birmingham Pals to die on the Somme.

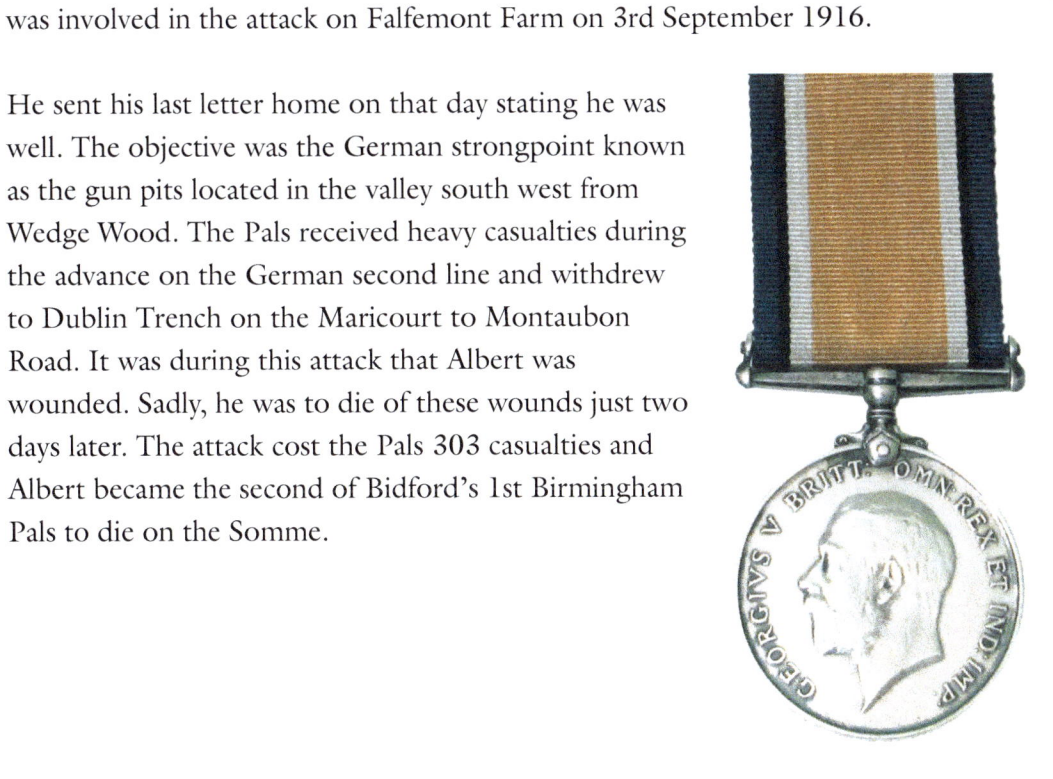

"We Will Remember Them"

Photograph: Don Mayrick

Thomas Mayrick
Private 17806, 14th Battalion,
(1st City of Birmingham)
Royal Warwickshire Regiment.
Died: Thursday 28th September 1916, aged 22
Buried in Bidford churchyard.
Medals: British and Victory medals.

Thomas Mayrick was the son of George and Jane Mayrick (nee Simons) of Salford Road, Bidford. He had two brothers, George and James. The census of 1911 gives his trade as a baker.

Thomas enlisted in the army on 6th April 1916 at Stratford. He did his basic training in Chiseldon in Wiltshire. On completion of this he joined his battalion in France in July 1916. When Thomas arrived, his battalion was involved in the Somme battles. He was in the attack on Wood Lane on 22nd July and Longueval on 30th July – the day that Fred McQuay was killed. On 3rd September the battalion was to launch an attack on German positions around Falfemont Farm and the objective was the gun pits in the valley south west from Wedge Wood. They sustained severe casualties on the advance to the second objective and withdrew to Dublin Trench on the Maricourt to Montaubon Road. It is most likely that this is when Thomas received his wounds. In the period of 19th July to 25th September 1916 his battalion sustained casualty figures of 36 officers and 1,004 other ranks.

After treatment at a casualty clearing station Thomas was sent to a base hospital near the coast and from there by

70

boat to Netley Military Hospital close to Southampton Water in Hampshire. He died a few days later on Thursday 28th September.

Upon news of his death, steps were taken at once to arrange if possible for burial to take place in Bidford. The request was consented to by the military authorities. On Saturday 30th September his body was conveyed by train to Leamington and here it was met by the bearer party consisting of Corporal R. Cowper (Warwickshire Yeomanry), Private Haywood (Royal Flying Corps), Private James Elsmore (Royal Warwickshire Regiment) and Private Fred Salisbury of the Gloucesters. The Evesham Journal reported, "The coffin covered with the Union Jack was placed on a motor chassis kindly lent by Mr Dennis of the White Lion hotel and made to appear like a gun carriage. It was then brought to Bidford and the procession formed up at the bottom of the village and included family, friends and companions of Thomas. The streets were thronged with people and all the house and shop blinds closed. On arrival at the churchyard, it was met by the vicar, the Reverend J. W. Evans, who took the service. As the church was entered, the organist (Mr A. H. Stone) played 'Oh Rest in the Lord' and when the procession left the church he played the Dead March from 'Saul'. At the graveside the choir sang the hymn, 'On the Resurrection Morning'. The Last Post was sounded over the grave by buglers of the Church Lads Brigade from Alcester. The coffin plate simply bore the name, number and date of death. Floral wreaths were placed by family and friends. The arrangements had been carried out by Mr H. Collins, the undertaker."

David Gardner

Driver T4/161185, Royal Army Service Corps.
Died: Saturday 21st October 1916, aged 19.
Buried in Bidford churchyard.
Medals: British and Victory medals.

David Gardner was the son of David and Mary Ann Gardner (nee Stephens) of the High Street, Bidford. He was shown in the 1911 census as being employed as a market gardener. He had three brothers and two sisters, one brother called Leonard who was living at home with him, and another brother, George, who was married and living in Redditch.

David joined the army in December 1915, enlisting in Stratford-upon-Avon. He joined the Army Service Corps and after training was sent to France in early 1916. While on duty in February 1916 he met with an accident; while hitching up an ammunition waggon he was hit in the back by the pole of the waggon. At first his injuries seemed slight but there were to be serious developments. Due to failing health, he was discharged from the army on medical grounds in June 1916. He returned to Bidford and worked for a time as a market gardener's labourer but sadly, after a long and painful illness, he died at home on 21st October 1916. His brother George was with him at the time of his death. The cause of death shown on the certificate was cancer of the hip and exhaustion.

Following a full military funeral, he was buried in Bidford churchyard and his grave is to be found on the left side of the churchyard as you walk up the path. As he had been discharged from the army, there is no mention of him in soldiers who died in the Great War and the Medal Index cards. Despite a war grave he is not shown in the Commonwealth War Graves records.

T4/161185 DRIVER
DAVID GARDNER
ROYAL ARMY SERVICE CORPS
21ST OCTOBER 1916 AGE 19
AT REST

"We Will Remember Them"

Christopher John Edkins
Private 11762, 2nd Battalion,
Oxford and Bucks Light Infantry.
Died: Monday 13th November 1916, aged 21.
Remembered with honour, Redan Ridge Cemetery,
Number 3, Beaumont-Hamel, France.
Medals: 1914-15 Star, British and Victory medals.

Pte. C. J. EDKINS,
Oxford & Bucks L.I.
(Killed.)

Christopher Edkins was the son of Ellen Edkins of Bidford-on-Avon. The census of 1911 shows him living at Steppes Piece with his mother and stepfather, Thomas Moore. He had two brothers and one step-sister and was employed as a farm labourer. He enlisted early in the war, joining up on the 1st September 1914 in Birmingham. He joined the Oxford and Bucks Light Infantry and was sent to Portsmouth for his basic training. On completion of this he went to France on 4th April 1915 as part of a draft for the 2nd Battalion. This was a pre-war regular army unit attached to the 2nd Division.

He took part in several actions in 1915 and in one of these was slightly wounded. In September 1915 he was recommended for the Distinguished Conduct Medal for rescuing an officer under fire. An article in the Evesham Journal states that he was awarded this though there was no official record of his receiving it. By early 1916 the battalion was in Bethune before moving to Festubert. In June, just before the Battle of the Somme, Lieutenant-Colonel Crosse became their new commanding officer, being with them for the next three years.

Christopher took part in several famous actions after the battalion arrived on the Somme on 20th July. These included the attacks on Waterlot Farm, Guillemont Station, Trones Wood and Beaumont-Hamel. On the evening of 12th November 1916 the battalion moved into assembly positions from where they had been at rest at the

Hotel de Ville in Mailly-Maillet. They were to launch an attack towards Beaumont Trench on Redan Ridge. This was during the last Battle of the Somme known as the Battle of the Ancre. It was during this attack the following morning that Christopher was killed, eleven days after celebrating his 21st birthday on 2nd November. Total casualties were 284 officers and men.

Christopher's headstone is a special memorial and the inscription says, "Known to be buried in this cemetery". This means that he is certainly buried in the cemetery but his exact grave location is unknown.

Redan Ridge Cemetery, Number 3, Beaumont-Hamel, France

"We Will Remember Them"

Richard George Hughes
Airman 2nd class, 33212,
22nd Class Kite Balloon Section
Royal Flying Corps.
Died: Tuesday 5th December 1916, aged 18.
Buried in Varennes Military Cemetery,
France (plot 1, row 6, grave 56).
Medals: 1914-15 Star, British and Victory medals.

Richard Hughes was the son of Richard and Ella Hughes of Broom. The census of 1911 mentions neither Richard nor his father as by then his mother was a widow. Her occupation was given as farmer and owner of Broom Farm. Richard would no doubt have been a schoolboy and it is probable that his mother was a landowner. He may well have been away at school.

Richard enlisted in June 1915, joining the Royal Flying Corps. He did his training at Aldershot and Lydde and on completion of this he was posted to the balloon section as airman, 2nd class.

He was sent to France in October 1916. On Sunday 3rd December 1916 he was acting as a motor cycle dispatch rider carrying dispatches from base to headquarters, when en route he had an accident which caused him to fall from his motorcycle. This resulted in his receiving serious injuries including a fractured skull, broken collar bone and broken ribs. He was taken to hospital but sadly died from these injuries two days later.

Richard, the victim of a tragic accident, was the last man from the parish to die in 1916.

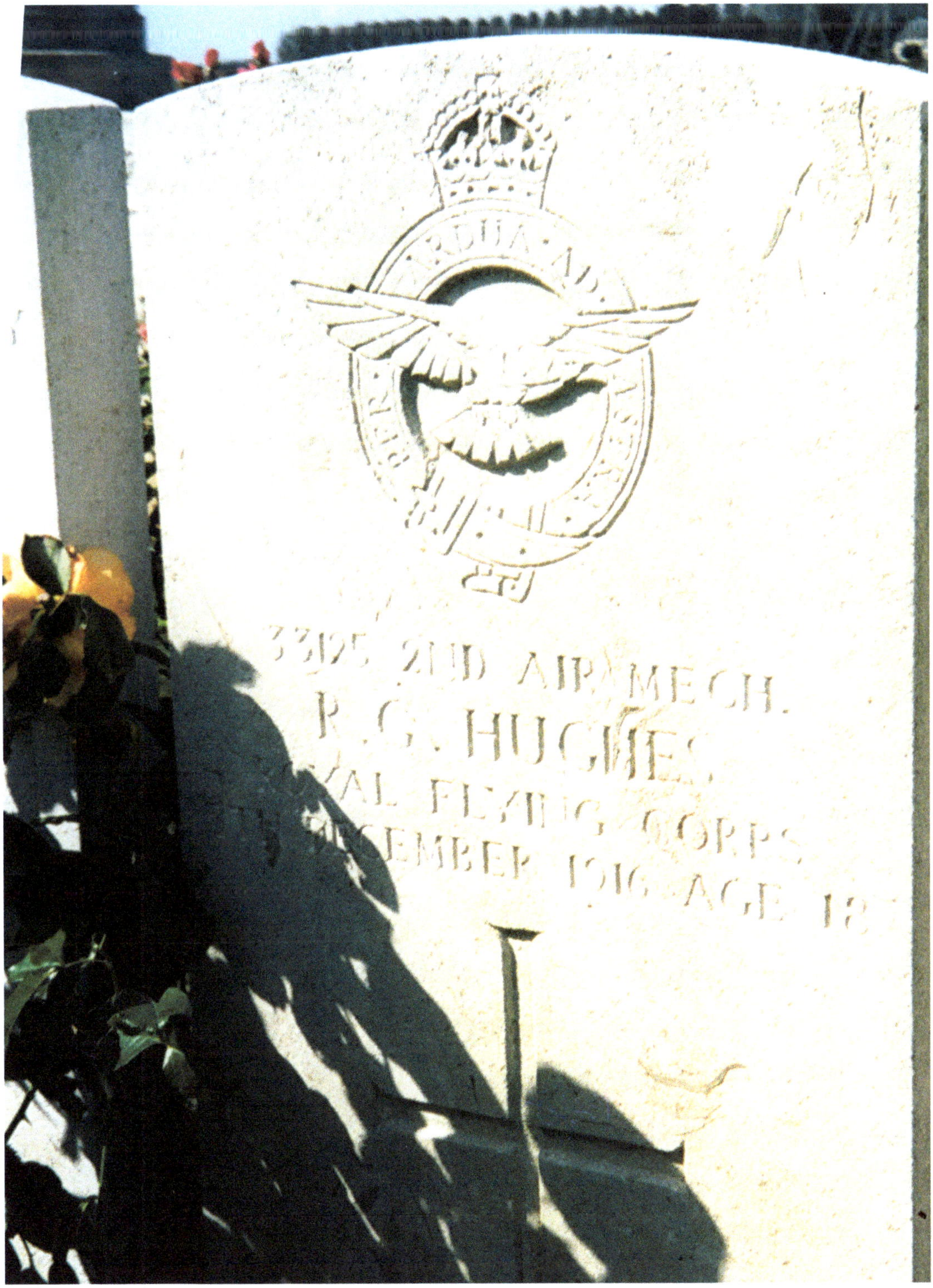
2ND AIR MECH.

"We Will Remember Them"

The Soldiers' Stories - 1917

The year 1917 was to prove the most costly for Bidford. Nineteen of her men were to give their lives during this year. Following months of attrition on the Somme during 1916, and with casualties of around 630,000, the Germans gave up their positions and withdrew to the fortress known as the Hindenburg Line.

The year would be remembered for three major offensives - the Battle of Arras which included the Canadians at Vimy Ridge, the third Battle of Ypres known as Passchendaele and the first mass use of tanks at the Battle of Cambrai in November 1917. It was a year in which three of Bidford's men were to die of ill health with April, being the worst month, when five of her men were lost. The losses, however, started very early in the New Year with Joe Bennett being killed in action on January 2nd. At the start of 1917, the war that had started in 1914 and would 'be over by Christmas' still had nearly 23 months to run.

Stretcher party at the Third Battle of Ypres (Passchendaele) 31 July-1st November 1917.
(Photograph courtesy of Imperial War Museum - Q 5935)

"We Will Remember Them"

William Rogers Bennett

Private 11812, D Company,
6th Battalion, Dorset Regiment.
Died: Tuesday 2nd January 1917, aged 23.
Buried in the Guards Cemetery, Les Boeufs,
France (plot 4, row A, grave 8).
Medals: 1914-15 Star,
British and Victory medals.

William Bennett, known locally as Joe, was the elder son of William and Amelia Bennett (nee Rogers) of Grange Road, Bidford. Joe was born in Bidford and had three sisters and one brother. Before the war he had been employed as a bricklayer's labourer.

He enlisted on 7th September 1914 at Birmingham Town Hall. He joined the Warwicks but was soon transferred to the Dorsets on 23rd October 1914. The Battalion had formed at Dorchester on 6th September 1914. He was sent to Wareham for training and then in May 1915 to Romsey in Hampshire.

He arrived in France at Boulogne on 14th July 1915. The year of 1915 found the battalion holding the line at the southern end of the Ypres Salient. On 9th February 1916 he was taken

80

Daily Mail Battle Pictures Series 1 No.1

by the 51st Field Ambulance to Number 17 Casualty Clearing Station suffering from influenza. On the 13th he re-joined his battalion. Three days later he was wounded in action, sustaining a gunshot wound to the left side of the chest. He was taken by the 52nd Field Ambulance to Number 10 Casualty Clearing Station. The following day he was admitted to Number 3 Canadian General Hospital at Boulogne and from there he was discharged to Marlborough for ten days.

He then returned to France and was sent to Etaples until he re-joined the battalion in the field on 23rd March 1916. In July the battalion was on the Somme taking part in the Battle of Albert. On 9th July Joe was admitted to Number 45 Casualty Clearing Station with influenza again. He was discharged on the 16th and sent to the depot at Rouen and re-joined the battalion on 5th August 1916, taking part in the Battle of Delville Wood. By January 1917 the battalion was still in trenches in the Somme region. Joe had been home on leave for six weeks prior to the New Year; it was the last time that his family saw him alive.

His parents received a letter from one of his officers informing them that Joe had been killed outright by a shell while acting as a company runner. He added that Joe had felt no pain whatsoever and had done sterling work.

"We Will Remember Them"

Norman Chester Reeves

Sergeant Farrier, 208635,
7th Field Troop, Royal Engineers.
Died: Wednesday 24th January 1917, aged 22.
Buried at Kantara War Memorial Cemetery,
Egypt (row A, grave 51).
Medals: 1914-15 Star, British and Victory medals.

Norman Reeves was the son of Mrs Ada Cantrill (formerly Reeves) of 84 West Street, Warwick and the late Charles Reeves. Norman himself had been born in King's Heath; however, the census of 1911 shows him living with his stepfather John at Vine Cottage, Salford Priors. Norman's occupation was given as blacksmith/general shoeing. Before the war Norman was living in Broom Road, Bidford and was employed by Mr Henry Mason as a blacksmith at his forge in Broom.

On 17th March 1912 he enlisted as Trooper 1869 in the Warwickshire Yeomanry. These were the part-time territorial soldiers. He had enlisted at Irons Cross and by the outbreak of war had reached the rank of Corporal Shoesmith. He was a member of D Squadron based in Stratford-upon-Avon, whose catchment area was Henley-in-Arden, Weston-sub-edge and Salford Priors.

When war began he was called up and moved on mobilisation to Bury-St-Edmunds as part of the 1st South Midland Mounted Brigade. On 31st August they

Photograph courtesy of Mick McCann of British War Graves

moved to Newbury joining the 2nd Mounted Division and in November 1914 they moved to Sherringham in Norfolk and on 17th December to Norwich. On 11th April 1915 Norman sailed from Avonmouth to Egypt on board 'The Wayfarer'. She was torpedoed 60 miles north west of the Scilly Isles and from there she was towed to Queenstown in Ireland. She finally arrived in Alexandria on 24th April 1915.

On 18th August 1915 Norman landed at Suvla Bay, Gallipoli as part of a dismounted unit. He took part in the attacks on Chocolate Hill and Hill 112 on 21st August. By early September 1915, due to sickness and battle casualties, they merged temporarily with the 1/1 Gloucestershire and 1/1 Worcestershire Yeomanry to form the first South Midland Regiment. They continued in trench warfare in the Green Hill and Chocolate Hill sectors until they were evacuated to Mudros, Greece on 31st October 1915. In December they withdrew completely from Gallipoli and returned to Egypt. On 21st April 1916 Norman was promoted to Sergeant Farrier and transferred into the 7th Field Troop Royal Engineers.

His mother received a letter in February 1917 informing her that Norman had died at the 24th Casualty Clearing Station on 24th January of para-typhoid which is caused by drinking unclean water.

Kantara War Memorial Cemetery, Egypt,
Photograph courtesy of Mick McCann of British War Graves

"We Will Remember Them"

William Francis Pulham
Driver T4/109800, 239th HT Company,
Army Service Corps.
Died: Saturday 17th March 1917, aged 53.
Buried in St Laurence's churchyard, Bidford.
Medals: 1914-15 Star, British and Victory medals.

William Pulham was born at Stow-on-the Wold and from Stow he moved to Bleachfield Street in Alcester. He and his wife Mary (nee Phipps) had a total of ten children, five daughters and five sons. During the war the family moved again, this time to the Falcon Buildings, Bidford. In civilian life, William was employed as a farm labourer.

William enlisted in the army on 1st May 1915 in Stratford-upon-Avon. Although over 50 years of age he was accepted into the Army Service Corps. He did his training at Aldershot, Royal Park and Codford St Mary. He asked for an overseas posting and went as a driver to France on 5th March 1916. In December 1916 he was returned to England suffering from rheumatism and shellshock. He was taken to Kemstone Military Hospital in Bedford for treatment. Sadly, he died there on 17th March 1917. He was brought back to Bidford for burial on Wednesday 21st March 1917.

The coffin was draped in the Union Jack and was accompanied by six soldiers who acted as bearers. The procession was met at the lych-gate by the vicar. There then followed a choral service after which they left the church to the Dead March from 'Saul' played on the organ. At the graveside, the Last Post was sounded by the Alcester Church Lads Brigade. Floral tributes were placed on the grave including one from the officers at Bedford. At the age of 53, William, along with George Leonard, were the oldest casualties from Bidford to die during the war. At the time of his death he had two sons in the army and one in the navy. One of the sons was to be killed the following year.

T4/109800 DRIVER
W. PULHAM
ROYAL ARMY SERVICE CORPS
17TH MARCH 1917

"We Will Remember Them"

Bernard Harold Pitcher

Lance Corporal 9249, 11th Battalion,
Royal Warwickshire Regiment.
Died: Tuesday 10th April 1917, aged 21.
Commemorated on the Arras Memorial,
France (bay 3).
Medals: 1914-15 Star, British and Victory medals.

Lce-Cpl. B. H. PITCHER,
Royal Warwicks.
Killed.

Bernard Pitcher was the son of Thomas and Ruth Pitcher (nee Hope) and was born in Pebworth. He had three brothers, Wilfred, Carl and Hubert, and a sister, Ruth. The census of 1911 shows the family having moved from Pebworth into the Falcon Buildings, Bidford. At the time Bernard was shown working as an errand boy.

Bernard enlisted in the army in November 1914 at Stratford-upon-Avon. He joined the 11th Warwickshire Battalion which was raised in September 1914 and was part of the 24th Division. It was to assemble at Shoreham but lacked officers, NCOs and equipment. As so many people had answered Kitchener's call, 'Your Country Needs You', the army was swamped and there were not enough to go round. Bernard therefore did most of his training in Warwick. In April 1915 the battalion was transferred to the 112th Brigade of the 27th Division and moved to Cholderton on Salisbury Plain. On 30th July they sailed to France, arriving the next day. They assembled near a place called Tilques. Bernard was not involved in any major battles until 1916 when the battalion fought at the final Somme attack known

Arras Memorial, France (bay 3)

as the Battle of the Ancre. By now he had been promoted to the rank of Lance Corporal and was a member of the battalion's machine gun section. In April 1917 the battalion took part in the Battle of the Scarpe which was part of the Battle of Arras which began on 9th April and ended on 16th May 1917. It was on the second day of fighting, 10th April, that Bernard was killed in action. By the time of Bernard's death the family had moved to 70 Charlotte Road, Stirchley, Birmingham. His younger brother Carl was to be killed in France a year later.

BIDFORD-ON-AVON BROTHERS KILLED.

Pte. C. R. PITCHER,
Wilts. Regt.
Missing now reported Killed.

Lce-Cpl. B. H. PITCHER,
Royal Warwicks.
Killed.

The above are the portraits of the sons of Mr. and Mrs. T. Pitcher, of Charlotte-road, Stirchley, Birmingham, and formerly of the Falcon Buildings, Bidford-on-Avon, both of whom lost their lives in the war. Pte. Carl Rudolph Pitcher enlisted in November, 1917, and was attached to the Wiltshire Regt. He went through his training on Salisbury Plain and went out to France in April, 1918.

He was reported wounded and missing on May 30, 1918, and is now officially reported to have been killed on that date. His brother Lance-Corpl. Bernard Harold Pitcher, joined the Royal Warwickshire Regt. in November, 1914, and was trained at Warwick. He went to France in May, 1915, and was killed in action on April 10, 1917.

An extract from the Evesham Journal, May 1919

Horace Frank Hartwell

Private 20326, 1st Battalion, Essex Regiment.
Died: Saturday 14th April 1917, aged 22.
Commemorated on the Arras Memorial,
France (bay 7).
Medals: 1914-15 Star, British and Victory medals.

Horace Hartwell was born in Broom, the son of Thomas and Julia Hartwell (nee Hodges). The census of 1911 shows the family living in Gashouse Cottages, Bidford. His sister Elsie was also living at home and he had four older brothers. Along with Elsie, there were two older sisters who were not living at home. His occupation was given as farm labourer. Prior to that, when leaving school, he had worked at Prickett's, the local butcher's in the High Street, Bidford.

He enlisted in Birmingham in September 1914 and joined as a private, number 11763, in the Oxford and Bucks Light Infantry. Following training he transferred into the Royal Field Artillery. In 1915 he went with his battery to Gallipoli and saw action there. While on the peninsula, Horace caught enteric fever and was invalided back to England.

After regaining his health, he was transferred to the Essex regiment and was posted to his battalion in France in early July 1916. He would have missed the opening of the Battle of the Somme which was fortunate for him as the Essex regiment was virtually wiped out on the first day of the battle at Newfoundland Park, Beaumont Hamel. In 1917 the battalion was in action in the Battle of Arras which began on 9th April 1917. It was during this battle that he was reported missing on 14th April 1917. His parents did not receive official confirmation of his death until January 1918. By then his older brother had been discharged from the army, having been wounded in the back.

The Soldiers' Stories - 1917

Bernard Houghton

Corporal 240580, 1st/8th Battalion, Worcestershire Regiment.
Died: Tuesday 24th April 1917, aged 26.
Commemorated on the Thiepval Memorial, France (piers 5 & 6, faces A & C).
Medals: British and Victory medals.

Bernard Houghton was the son of Henry and Sarah Houghton (nee Addis). His mother came from Badsey and he had four older brothers. The 1911 census shows him living at 5 Philips Terrace, Besley Road, Redditch. He was employed in the needle industry working as a needle scourer. Living with him was his wife Lavinia (nee Houghton) who had been born in Bidford.

Bernard enlisted in the army at Worcester. This would have been after 1915 as he did not receive the 1914-15 Star. The 1st/8th Worcesters had been formed in August 1914 and had trained at Maldon before embarking for France on 31st March 1915. They became part of the 48th South Midland Division. The battalion was involved in action during the Battle of the Somme at the Quadrilateral Bazentine Ridge, Ovillers, Pozieres, Ancre Heights and the Battle of the Ancre. In 1917 they were involved in actions during the German retreat to the Hindenberg Line. As there is no known date of his enlistment, we cannot speculate about his movement or actions prior to his death. What is certain, however, is where he was at the time of being killed in action, the information coming from the battalion diary. On 24th April 1917 the battalion was in position ready to attack Guillemont Farm in the Somme region. They had moved up from the rest area at Templeux-le-Guerard the previous day. At 3.45 am on the 24th, A, C, and D companies were to attack the farm. Following this action, a roll call found the battalion had sustained a total of 160 casualties and Bernard was amongst those killed. His body was never found.

Panel extract from Thiepval Memorial.
Photograph from Mick McCann
of British War Graves

Frederick George Smith

Lance Corporal, 17017,
7th Battalion, Wiltshire Regiment.
Died: Wednesday 25th April 1917, aged 20.
Buried at Dorian Military Cemetery,
Greece (plot 3, row D, grave 5).
Medals: 1914-15 Star, British and Victory medals.

Frederick Smith was the son of Esther Collett (formerly Smith, her maiden name had been Parry and she came from Childswickham) of Alcester Road, Bidford and the late John Smith. Fred's place of birth was Stanley Bontlarge. He was a single man living with his mother before the war and in 1911 aged 14, he was employed as a groom and domestic servant working at the Dolphin Inn, Bishampton for Mr Eustace Meadows. He had four brothers and two sisters.

When war broke out he enlisted in the army aged just 17 on 22nd September 1914 at Stratford-upon-Avon. He originally enlisted as 15331 in the Oxford and Bucks Light Infantry, but was then transferred into the Wiltshire regiment and was sent to Codford and Marlborough for training.

It was not until early 1915, however, that they got any proper uniforms owing to the shortages of khaki material. In April they moved to Sutton Veny for final training. Frederick sailed to France in September 1915 where the battalion concentrated at Guignemicourt west of Amiens.

The Soldiers' Stories - 1917

"Since going to France in September 1915 Fred had not been home on leave."

Their stay in France, however, was short and in November 1915 they sailed to Salonika via Marseilles. On 26th December 1915 they moved from Lembet (Salonika) to Happy Valley camp. In 1916 Fred would have taken part in the Battle of Horseshoe Hill. During this time he had been promoted to Lance Corporal. In 1917 he took part in the Battle of Doiran. The Bulgarians had 30,000 men in defensive positions with 147 guns, 130 machine guns and 35 mortars. The British had 43,000 men, 160 guns, 440 machine guns and 110 mortars. The battle raged from 22nd April 1917 until 8th May. The artillery barrage began on 22nd April and the infantry attack went in on the 24th.

Fred's mother received official notification that he had been killed in action during an attack on the Bulgarian trenches between 24th and 25th April 1917. By the end of the battle the Bulgarians had lost 2,000 men and the British 12,000. Since going to France in September 1915 Fred had not been home on leave.

Doiran Military Cemetery, Greece

"We Will Remember Them"

Frank Hancocks
Private, 438018, 8th Battalion,
Canadian Infantry (Manitoba) Regiment.
Died: Saturday 28th April 1917, aged 28.
Commemorated on the
Vimy Ridge Memorial, France.
Medals: 1914-15 Star, British and Victory medals.

Frank Hancocks was born on 2nd April 1889 in Birmingham. One of nine children, he was the son of Maria Harbige of Waterloo Cottage, Bidford and the late William Hancocks. His stepfather was Alfred Harbige who was a beer retailer and Frank also had a step-brother Albert. At some stage he had emigrated to Canada where he worked as a lineman. He also spent time in the militia serving with the 15th Light Horse of Alberta.

He enlisted on 18th December 1914 into the 52nd Canadian Infantry Battalion at Port Arthur. Following training, he sailed from Montreal on 17th June 1915 aboard the S.S. Scandinavian. On arriving in England he was taken on strength by the Canadian army at Shorncliffe. He was passed fit for duty on 2nd August 1915 and on 14th August he arrived in France as part of the 8th Battalion draft, known as the Black Devils, but he was soon to suffer, with ill health due to many attacks of haemorrhoids over nearly a 12 month period. This resulted in his having an operation in July 1916 and he was first admitted to Moore Barracks, Shorncliffe before being sent to Bearwood, Wokingham and finally to Woodcote in Epsom for convalescence. He was passed fit for duty by a medical board on 15th November 1916 and sailed for France on 28th December 1916. He was taken on strength the next day and went straight into the field.

On 28th April the battalion was involved in an attack on Arleux not far from Vimy Ridge. Following a barrage at 4.25am the attack went in. By 5.15am good progress was being made; however, they then met with heavy opposition in the town and from a

Frank Hancocks commemorated on the Vimy Ridge Memorial, France

nearby wood. This was caused by heavy machine gun fire and snipers. The objectives were finally reached and held by 8.00am. Many German prisoners were taken and put to use as stretcher-bearers. The Germans counter-attacked at 8.35pm and again at 4.00am on the 29th. During the night of the 28th the Germans fired many shells on Arleux including gas. Battalion casualties for this action were 4 officers killed and 4 wounded, 50 other ranks killed, 200 wounded and 50 missing. Frank was one of the missing and his body was never found but his death was reported in the Birmingham Daily Post four months later.[10]

8th Battalion marching to the front with General Byng taking the salute

10. *Birmingham Daily Post, 13th August 1917*

"We Will Remember Them"

Lewis Stanford

Private 2349, 5th Battalion,
Oxford and Bucks Light Infantry.
Died: Thursday 3rd May 1917, aged 24.
Commemorated on the Arras Memorial,
France (bays 6 & 7).
Medals: 1914-15 Star, British and Victory medals.

Lewis Stanford was the son of Henry Thomas and Julia Stanford (nee James). He was one of six children and had been born at Buckland in Gloucestershire. The census of 1911 shows him living at home with his parents and a sister called Alma. By then the family was living in Broom. His father was a car driver for the mill and was employed by Mr F. J. Adkins. Lewis, or 'Jack' as he was known locally, was employed as a miller. At the outbreak of the war he went with several others from Broom to Birmingham by car to enlist (see opposite page). He joined the 5th Oxford and Bucks which had been formed in August 1914 in Oxford. The main part of the battalion landed in France on 21st May 1915 after completing its training at Portsmouth. Lewis had gone out earlier

Lewis Stanford commemorated on the Arras Memorial, France.
Photograph courtesy of Mick McCann, British War Graves

The Soldiers' Stories - 1917

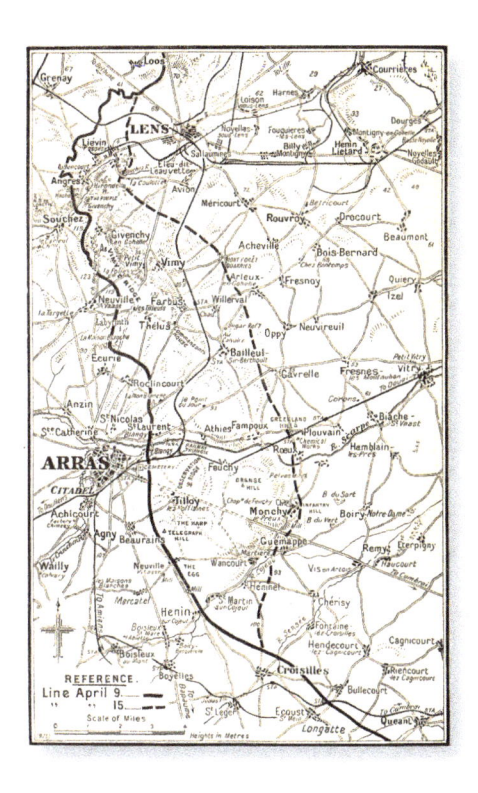

with an advance party on 1st May 1915. He took part in fighting at Hooge in Belgium on 30th July when the Germans used flame throwers for the first time. On 1st September he was at Vlamertinghe and on the 16th, west of Poperinghe (map reference 27). On 26th September they were in bivouacs in a field at La Lovil Chateau near Poperinghe again, having been badly mauled at the second Battle of Bellewarde. The 13th October found them in trenches at Railway Wood. By 1916 they were on the Somme and on 2nd August Lewis was wounded in fighting at Delville Wood. Because of his wounds, he was sent to hospital in Devizes in Wiltshire to recover. He came home on leave in March 1917 prior to returning to France.

He was with his battalion during an attack on 3rd May 1917 on a position known as New Trench. This was during the Battle of Arras. His parents received a letter from his commanding officer saying that he was missing and might be a prisoner-of-war. A letter from the War Office, however, confirmed his death. The battalion lost 300 men that day.

Map above: Area of operations for the Oxford and Bucks Light Infantry April 1917.

Pictured right: The men from Broom going to enlist in 1914. Pictured third from the left, Arthur Hartland and fourth from left, Lewis Stanford.

"We Will Remember Them"

William John Henry Payne
Private 19336,
2nd Battalion, Royal Warwickshire Regiment.
Died: Friday 4th May 1917, aged 20.
Commemorated on the Arras Memorial,
France (Bay 3).
Medals: British and Victory medals.

William Payne was the eldest son of Henry and Rebecca Payne (nee Hopkins) of Barton. The family home was in one of the two cottages just before the turning to Dorsington. William was born at Wick in Worcestershire and had two brothers, Ernest and Percy, and an older sister, Primrose. The census of 1911 shows him living at Hinton on the Green and added to the family was a 5 month old sister, Dorothy. It shows him at the age of 14 working as a domestic gardener. By the age of 18 he had married a widow, Emily Steele, and they had gone to live at Lillbourne near Rugby. William took up employment as a domestic servant.

William joined the army in May 1916, enlisting at Rugby. Following completion of his training he was posted to France with the 2nd Battalion of the

The railway embankment which ran parallel to the Hindenburg Line south east of Bullecourt. Photographer: Herbert Frederick Baldwin, 8 May 1917
Courtesy of: www.awm.gov.au

The Hindenburg Line at Bullecourt. Three trench lines and communications are here shown, with acres of wire entanglements in the left foreground protecting first-line positions.
(Photograph taken 1920) Photograph courtesy of Wikimedia Commons.

Warwickshire Regiment in December of that year. In May 1917 the battalion was in position at Mory Copse near to Bullecourt in support of the 1st Anzac Corps who were due to attack the Germans' Hindenburg Line. The attack went in on 3rd May but the Warwicks were held in reserve in a railway cutting. On that day they were not used as the Anzac attack was a failure. The following day, the 4th, the attack was to take place on Bullecourt itself. The Warwicks were to leave the railway cutting at 12.30am and attack over open ground at 3.45am, north east of Ecoust.

Sometime after the battle, William's wife Emily was notified that he was missing, believed killed in action during the attack of 4th May 1917. His body was never found and Emily became a widow for the second time. His brother, Ernest, was amongst those who survived the war and is included in the list at the end of this book.

"We Will Remember Them"

Walter William Taylor
Lance Corporal 17178,
1st Battalion, Hampshire Regiment.
Died: Saturday 12th May 1917, aged 30.
Buried at Pont-de-Jours Military Cemetery,
France. (Plot 1, row J, grave 5).
Medals: 1914-15 Star, British and Victory medals.

Walter Taylor was the eldest son of Joseph and Jane Taylor (nee Lane) of Barton. Walter had been born at Littleton Pastures. Before the war, like his father, he worked as a farm labourer, his father driving the farm carts. He had three brothers and two sisters.

Walter was an early volunteer, enlisting in Birmingham in September 1914 along with his brother Thomas and their friend William Bott. They all enlisted in the Oxford and Bucks Light Infantry and Walter's regimental number was 12776. He was then transferred to the 2nd Hampshires and went with them to Gallipoli in June 1915. He did not, however, remain there for too long as he became ill with fever and dysentery. He was evacuated via Egypt back to England where he recovered in a Manchester hospital.

On returning to full health, he was posted to France on 21st March 1916 with the 1st Battalion Hampshire Regiment. Here he took part in the opening battle of the Somme. The battalion's objectives on 1st July were Beaumont Hamel, Y Ravine and Hawthorn Ridge. Owing to the heavy casualties of other battalions, however, especially the Newfoundlanders, the Hampshires' attack at noon was called off. William also took part in the Battle of Transloy. In April 1917 the battalion was involved at Arras at the Battle of the Scarp from the 9th to the 14th April, the third Battle of the Scarp on the 3rd and 4th May and the capture of Fresnoy and Roeux. It was during this campaign that Walter was killed on 12th May serving in the battalion's Lewis gun section.

The Soldiers' Stories - 1917

Photograph: Doreen Bird

"We Will Remember Them"

Frederick Mark Bennett
Private 4738, 15th (King's) Hussars.
Died: Saturday 13th June 1917 aged 32.
Buried at La Targette British Cemetery, France.
Medals: Mons Star, British and Victory medals.

Fred Bennett was born in Bidford. He was the third son of the late Abel and Sarah Bennett. He had seven brothers and one sister. By the time of Fred's death his mother had moved from Salford Road to Flecknoe near Rugby. Fred was a single man who had seen service as a regular soldier. In the 1911 census he was serving with the Hussars in the Transvaal in South Africa and was stationed at Potchefstroom. On leaving the army he was employed by Bomford and Evershed at Salford Priors and his job entailed travelling around the local area dredging rivers.

On leaving the army he had been placed on the reserve and was called back to the colours as soon as war was declared. His original place of enlistment had been at Alcester. He landed in France on 23rd August 1914 and was badly wounded during the Battle of Mons. He was sent back to England to recover from his injuries and did not return to France until January 1917. He was killed just six months later.

His mother received a letter from an old army pal of Fred's, Albert Richardson, with whom he had served in South Africa. In it he told her how Fred had met his death. He said they had been digging trenches early in the morning when a shell had burst overhead, rendering Fred unconscious. He had been severely wounded in the jaw and breast. He was removed from the line but sadly died before he could reach hospital. At the time of his death five of his brothers were also in the army, three in France, one in Africa and one training at Catford. There is a note on his medal index card from the I/C of the cavalry records on 6th January 1922. It asks for the authority to dispose of his medals as it would appear that the family was so upset by his death that they did not want them.

Michael Charles Finnemore

Rifleman A/3308,
12th Battalion, King's Royal Rifle Corps.
Died: Tuesday 21st August 1917, aged 26.
Buried at Harlebeke New British Cemetery, Belgium.
Medals: 1914-15 Star, British and Victory medals.

Michael Finnemore was the son of Michael Charles and Elizabeth Ann Finnemore (nee Luton) of Marlcliff. He was born in Aston, Birmingham and was a machine toolmaker as was his father. Michael had four brothers, Louis, Charles, Bernard and Anthony and one sister called Zita. In 1901 the family was shown as living at 58 Deykins Avenue, Erdington.

Michael enlisted during 1914 at Birmingham, joining the King's Royal Rifle Corps. In November 1914 the battalion was at Blackdown before moving to Hindhead in February 1915 and on to Larkhill in April. The battalion landed at Boulogne on 21st July 1915. It must be assumed that Michael was in the advance party as his medal index card shows him arriving in France on 19th May 1915. August 1915 shows him in the Fauquissart sector at Bethune and attacking Fauquissart itself on 25th September 1915. From January to June 1916 Michael was in the Ypres sector and would have been involved in action at Mount Sorrell on 13th June 1916. From July to October 1916 he would have seen action on the Somme. January 1917 found him in the Morval sector of the Somme, then in March in the advance to Metz and Bertincourt. In June the battalion was in the Arras sector to the north of Lagnicourt and from here they returned to the Ypres Salient. The War Graves Commission records him as dying here from disease on 21st August 1917. Sadly, his death was not recorded by the army so the Register of Births and Deaths does not have a copy of a death certificate, meaning the actual cause is unknown. On the day he died, the weather on the Salient was dry for once, temperature 72F, clear and with no rainfall.

Samuel Churchley
Corporal 63401,
94th Field Company, Royal Engineers.
Died: Thursday 20th September 1917, aged 36.
Buried at Oxford Road Cemetery, Ypres, Belgium
(plot 1, row H, grave 20).
Medals: 1914-15 Star, British and Victory medals.

Samuel Churchley was born in Bidford, the son of Harry and Elizabeth Churchley (nee Taylor). He had one brother and three sisters. Later in life he moved to Evesham with his wife, Hilda May (nee Tredwell) and they set up home at 15 Burford Road, Bengeworth. The census of 1911 shows them having two sons, William and Edward, but by the time of his death they had three more children aged from eleven to the youngest aged two. In civilian life Samuel worked as a bricklayer for Mr C. Knott of Evesham.

Samuel enlisted in the Royal Engineers at Evesham on 20th January 1915. On completion of his training he was sent to France on 20th July 1915. Nothing is known of his movements from then until he was wounded on 23rd July 1917. He came home on leave in August for ten days to aid his recovery.

Within a few weeks of returning to the Front he was killed outright in the mud and horror of Passchendaele during the battle for the Menin Road Ridge. On this day the temperature

Battle of Menin Road - wounded on the Menin Road, near Birr Cross Road

was 66F and was overcast. Shortly after his death his wife received a letter from his company commander, Captain W. Murray MacDonald. He wrote,

'Dear Mrs Churchley, It is with deep regret that I write to inform you of the death of your husband on 20/9/17. It will be some consolation for you to know he was killed instantly so suffered no pain, also that he made the supreme sacrifice and has given of his best and that you have also made noble sacrifice in giving him to your country. Your husband was one of the best and most reliable of my non-coms in the company and was thought a great deal of by all his officers and men of the company. He will be greatly missed by all of 94th Field Company. His personal belongings will be sent to you and I trust will be safely received. Your husband was buried by men of his section and I hope I will be able to let you have the exact location of the cemetery where he is buried at a later date. With heartfelt sympathy in which the whole company joins for you and your children in the very great loss you bear.
W. Murray MacDonald, Captain, R.E.'

"We Will Remember Them"

Ernest Ash

Private 88497,
11th Company, Machine Gun Corps (Infantry).
Died: Thursday 4th October 1917, aged 19.
Commemorated on the Tyne Cot Memorial, Belgium.
Medals: British and Victory medals.

Ernest Ash was the son of Edward and Martha Ash of Salford Road, Bidford. Ernest was born at Nottgrove in Gloucestershire where his father was a farm labourer. Ernest had three brothers and five sisters. They ranged in age from 21 to two. Before the war Ernest was employed as a grocery assistant working at the Bidford Co-operative shop situated in the High Street.

Ernest enlisted in the army on 2nd December 1916 with the 11th Company Machine Gun Corps. He did his basic training at Chistledon in Wiltshire and during his training he celebrated his 19th birthday on 20th March 1917. On completing his machine gun training he was posted to France, landing in Boulogne on 14th May 1917. He joined his company in the field on 22nd May 1917 having gone via the base depot at Comiers. He moved up to the front with his company for the third Battle of Ypres, better known as Passchendaele. He took part in the Battle of Polygon Wood before being killed in the Battle of Broodseinde. That day the temperature was 60F, overcast and with 4.6mm of rain.

Several months after his death a letter was received by his parents from his company commander informing them of how Ernest had died. He told them that their son had been the number one in charge of gun 2C. Ernest's job had been to fire the gun. At about twelve noon on the 4th October Ernest had been wounded in the foot by a piece of shrapnel while getting the gun out of action. His C.O. noticed that Ernest was having problems trying to walk. With the aid of two men they carried him towards a pillbox with a concrete emplacement nearby. Before getting there an 8 inch shell exploded between the four of them and the pillbox. Ernest was killed instantly by a piece of shrapnel through the heart. Another man was killed and a third was blown on top of the pillbox, smashing his foot. The officer himself had been knocked out and was out of action for several hours with a slight wound. He had notified the Graves Commission who would erect a cross in Ernest's memory. Only eight out of 40 in the company had come out unscathed. Ernest was buried beside the German pillbox located between Langemarck and Poelcapple. After much shelling of the area his body was never found.

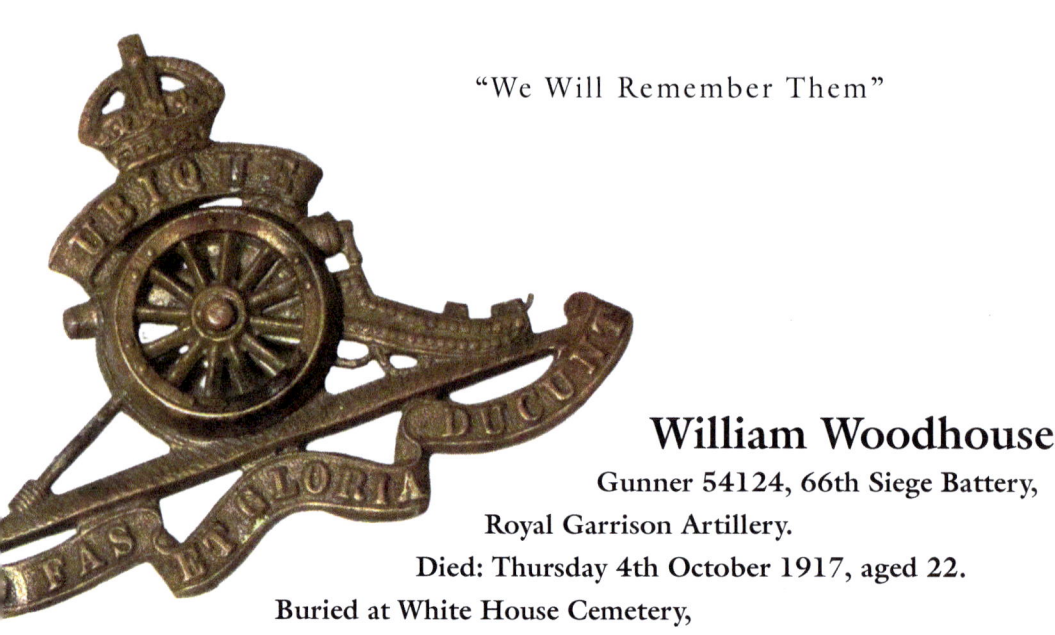

"We Will Remember Them"

William Woodhouse
Gunner 54124, 66th Siege Battery,
Royal Garrison Artillery.
Died: Thursday 4th October 1917, aged 22.
Buried at White House Cemetery,
St Jean-les-Ypres, Belgium (plot 2, row B, grave 14).
Medals: 1914-15 Star, British and Victory medals.

William Woodhouse was born at Stuckley in Worcestershire. Before the war he was living in Birmingham and was employed by Cadbury's of Bourneville.

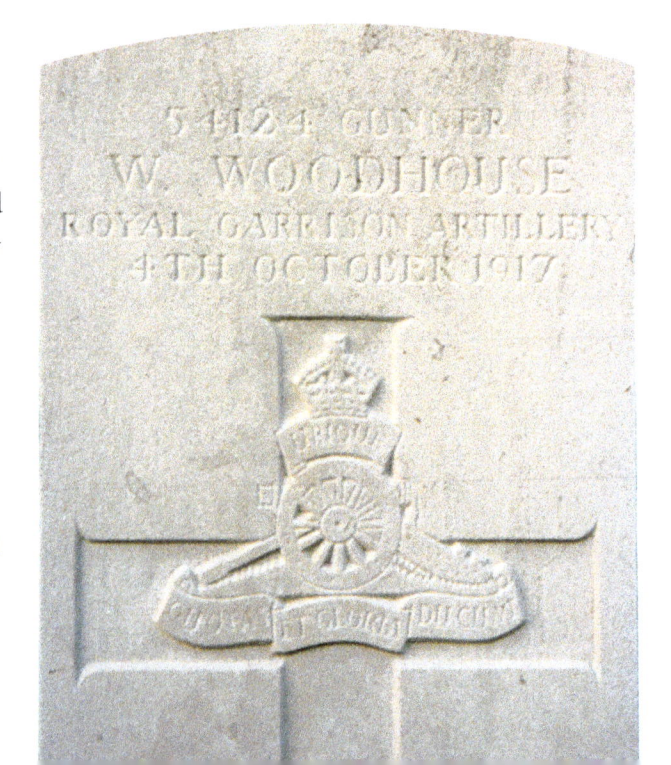

William enlisted in the artillery on 26th November 1914 at Suffolk Street in Birmingham. He was sent down to Plymouth for his basic training and on completion of this he was sent to France on 22nd July 1915. He joined his battery in the field on 7th August 1915 before returning to base on 28th September. On 4th October he sailed from Le Havre back to England. While in England he married Rose Ellen Richardson of Bidford on 10th February 1916. The two witnesses were Mrs Dance and Maud Seymour whose husband John had been killed in 1915. They had one child, Jesse, who was born in Alcester on 1st October 1916. The couple had set up home on Tower Hill, Bidford. He returned to France on 18th March 1916, sailing from Folkestone. He was in hospital for a day on 13th June and again on 28th September because of accidental injuries. From then until 5th August 1917 when he went home on leave, most of his time was spent between base and in the field. Following his leave, he returned to France on 15th August 1917. He re-joined his battery which was by then in action in the third Battle of Ypres at the Battle of Broodseinde.

The next news his wife received was to inform her that he had been killed in action on 4th October 1917. It is most probable the gun had received a direct hit as he is buried next to his comrades. They were Gunner Ahern (aged 43 from Youghal, County Cork), Sergeant W. Barry (aged 28, from Tullamore, King's County), Gunner W. A. Clarke, Battery Sergeant Major F. H. Makey DCM (aged 39, from Gosport, Hampshire), Gunner A. Lockhart (aged 32, from North Berwick, East Lothian), Gunner G. Riddleston (aged 31, from New Cross, London) and 2nd Lieutenant W. C. Jenkins. Ernest Ash also died on the same day.

In February 1918 his wife received his disc and some photographs he had with him when he was killed. On 22nd April 1918 she was granted a widow's pension of 18/-9d for herself and her child whom William had only known for ten days. In August 1921 she received the Great War and Victory medals but did not get his 1914-15 Star until September 1949!

6-inch gun of the Royal Garrison Artillery firing at night

Photograph: Library and Archives Canada. no. 3194805

"We Will Remember Them"

Samuel Frederick Baker Blackwell DSO

Captain, 9th (Service) Battalion Norfolk Regiment.
Died: Tuesday 20th November 1917, aged 29.
Buried at Ribecourt British Cemetery,
France (plot 1, row B, grave 1). Commemorated
on a brass plaque inside Bidford church.
Medals: DSO, Mons Star, British and Victory medals.

Samuel Blackwell was born on 29th May 1888, the second son of Samuel Fowler Blackwell and Rosetta Mary Blackwell (nee Baker) of Bickmarsh Hall, Welford. Before the war Samuel was farming his own land at Charingworth. In 1911 he was still living at Bickmarsh with his sister Margaret. As a point of interest, the 1901 census shows him boarding in Bedford with Leecroft Freer and his family.

Samuel enlisted at the beginning of the war, joining the Royal Scots Greys. He went to France in November 1914, serving as a dispatch rider. On his return from France he was transferred to the East Kent Yeomanry, being commissioned as a temporary 2nd Lieutenant on 15th May 1915. He sailed with the regiment from Liverpool on 25th September aboard the Olympic to Gallipoli via Lemnos. He arrived at Helles on 8th October 1915 and here he remained as part of the 42nd (East Lancashire) Division until the battalion was evacuated from V Beach on the night of 30th December 1915. He was at this time described by a fellow officer as one of the bravest bombing officers and much admired by his men. In 1916 he transferred to the 9th Norfolks and while serving with them he won the DSO on 10th October 1916. At this time the battalion was in action on the Somme.

The following is an extract from the brigade diary written by Colonel Prior regarding the holding of Mild Trench by the Gueudecourt Road. *The garrison holding the trench, despite a good many casualties, were in the best of spirits. Blackwell was the life and soul of the party and*

The Soldiers' Stories - 1917

had carried out his work admirably. He had put a block in his right flank, on the left was the Gueudecourt Road on the other side of which were the Hampshires.' A further entry from 2nd Lieutenant A. T. K. Cubitt goes on to say the following: *'During a German attack I saw an officer and four men crawling towards me under heavy fire. Two of the men were killed but the officer (Lieutenant Blackwell) got there with two other men. He took over and I went to sleep in the mud.'* They fought for 48 hours with water up to their knees, soaked to the skin, practically no water to drink and dead beat. Blackwell put up his periscope to have a look around and got a bullet through it. Turning it upside down he put it up again only to have that end smashed by another bullet. They were finally relieved towards midnight on 19th October having held the trench for ten days. For his part in the action, Samuel was awarded the DSO.

By 1917 he had been promoted to the rank of captain. He had been slightly wounded in a raid on German positions in June 1917. Colonel Prior then goes on to tell us of the last time he saw Samuel alive, during an attack on Ribecourt during the Battle of Cambrai in November 1917. He says, *'In the advance we came across Blackwell with D Company. He informed me that Cuthbert and Cubitt had both been wounded and that he himself was hit but would carry on. That was the last time I saw him alive for he was killed later on'*. When the doctor examined the body he found that the first wound was a terrible one, despite which Samuel had continued to lead his company. He had crossed the Hindenberg Line and initiated the final attack against the last objective before being shot dead.

He had applied for a transfer to the Tank Corps which had been accepted but sadly he was killed before he could take up his new post.

Nathan Locke

Private 38274, 2nd Battalion (Princess Charlotte of Wales) Royal Berkshire Regiment.
Died: Sunday 2nd December 1917, aged 28.
Commemorated on the Tyne Cot Memorial, Belgium (panels 105 -106).
Medals: British and Victory medals.

Nathan Locke was the son of James and Mary Locke (nee Sheppard). His father, who was from Minster Lovel, was a shepherd and his mother came from Stow-on-the-Wold. They had four sons serving in the armed forces and the Evesham Journal published an article about this in February 1918, describing them as a 'Patriotic Bidford Family'.

Nathan had five brothers; the eldest, Private George Lock, was born in Cleeve Prior in 1879 and joined the army in 1917 serving with the Army Service Corps in East Africa. The second son, Private Harry (Henry, also known as 'Paddy') Locke, lived at 8 Salford Road, Bidford and enlisted in London in January 1900 with the Notts and Derby Regiment, the 1st Sherwood Foresters, and served with the regiment in the Allied Forces in Peking, northern China. He was a reservist at the outbreak of war and went to France immediately with the Royal Warwickshire Regiment. He was at the retreat of Mons and many other engagements. As a time-expired man, he came home in December 1915 and re-joined the army in June 1916, then returning to France with the Warwicks. Paddy not only survived the war, but later unveiled Bidford's War Memorial in 1923.

He had two other brothers, Charles and Albert, as well as two sisters. The 1911 census shows Nathan as living with his parents and being employed as a painter. By 1917 Nathan was married with two children.

Nathan joined the army in October 1916, enlisting in Birmingham. He initially joined the Warwicks with an army number of 21531 but he did not remain with them long as he volunteered for the Tank Corps. He was posted to Wareham in Dorset where he was trained in the use of tanks. On completion of his training he was posted to France in May 1917 and served some time with the tanks before he was transferred to the Berkshire Regiment. He was with his battalion at the closing stages of the third Battle of Ypres. Depending on when he joined his battalion, he may well have been involved in the Battles of Pilkem Ridge and Langemarck. By late November they were located at Ridge Camp.

His wife then received a letter from his company commander informing her of Nathan's death. He said her husband had been killed instantly by a shell during an attack on German positions. He said that he had a cheerful and ready manner in which the deceased always did his duty. He added that his comrades had asked that he would express their deepest sympathy to her.

William Henry Liddell

Private 32835, 2/5th Battalion, Gloucestershire Regiment.
Died: Wednesday 5th December 1917, aged 21.
Buried at Sunken Road Cemetery, Villers-Plouich, France (row A, grave 4).
Medals: British and Victory medals.

William Liddell was the eldest son of William and Annie Liddell (nee Albutt) of Brook Leys, Bickmarsh. William was born at Belbroughton in Worcestershire. He had two brothers, Francis and Ernie and a sister, Elsie. He was employed as a ploughboy by Mr W. Smith of Clayhall Farm, Bickmarsh. His father was employed as a gamekeeper.

William enlisted into the 2/5th Gloucesters in Birmingham in January 1917. It was a territorial regiment. He went down to Sittingbourne in Kent to do his basic training and joined his battalion in the field in mid July 1917. He took part in the third Battle of Ypres. By October 1917 he was in trenches at the chemical works at Fampoux which is east of Arras. He then was involved in the Battle of Cambrai. By early December the battalion was in positions near to Villers Plouich and here he was wounded in action during counter-attacks by the Germans who were trying to consolidate the Front Line for the winter. Sadly, he died of his wounds on 5th December. His parents did not receive news of his death until, of all days, Christmas Day, 1917. He was buried in a small cemetery near where he died which contains just fifty graves and is located about one mile from the main village.

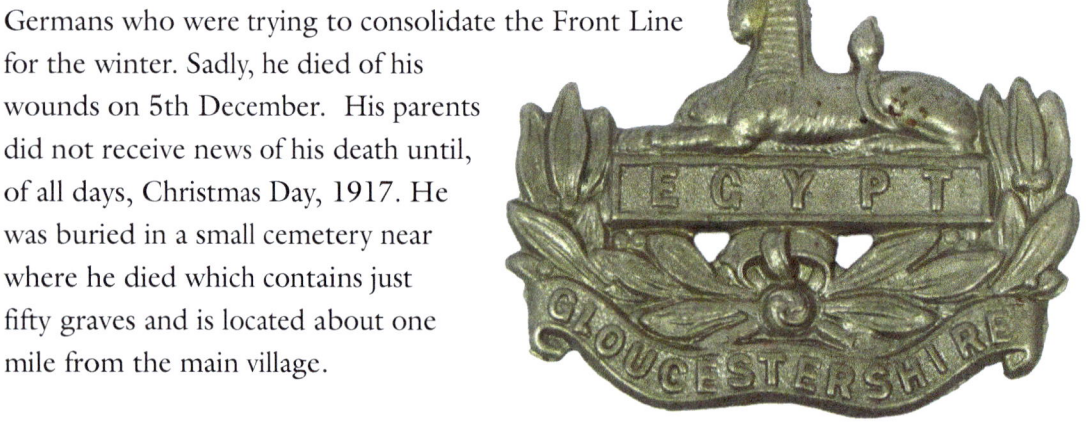

The Soldiers' Stories - 1917

*William was the last Bidford man
to lose his life in 1917,
a year which proved to be the deadliest of the war for the village.*

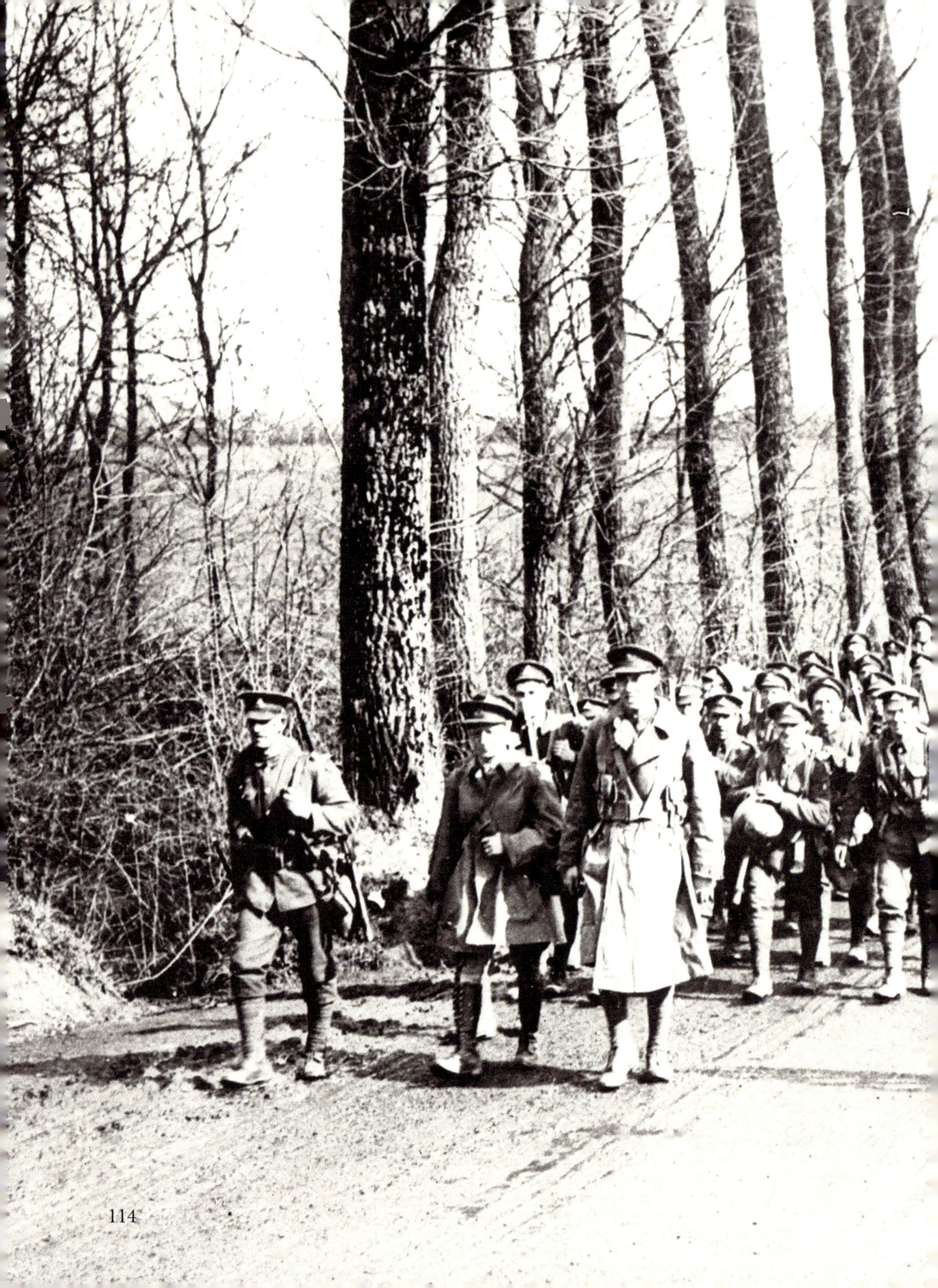

The Soldiers' Stories - 1918-1922

1918-1922

Following the awful slaughter of 1917, many people were wondering what the next year would bring. The first few months were fairly quiet with no major actions but following the revolution in Russia in 1917, the Russians pulled out of the war, freeing many German divisions to be moved from the eastern to the western front. The Germans were preparing for one final push, hoping to end the war and bring final victory. Meanwhile, Sir Douglas Haig went to London to ask the Prime Minister, Lloyd George, for more troops to be sent to France. He was denied this request and a few weeks later on 21st March the Germans attacked. It was known as 'Operation Michael' or 'Der Kaiserschlacht' and it nearly succeeded. The Germans used storm troopers and instead of taking every strong point, they by-passed them, leaving the follow-up waves to deal with them. Haig issued his order of 'no retreat' and to 'fight to the last man'. The first man to die from Bidford in 1918 was Cecil Pulham of the Machine Gun Corps and he died on the opening day of the German attack.

By August 1918, however, the tide had turned. The Germans were worn out, lacking in supplies and with trouble back in Germany, they could not withstand the allied counter-attack which now included the Americans. Within a hundred days the war ended on 11th November at 11 o'clock. The last battlefield casualty for Bidford was young Gerald Gould, aged just eighteen, killed three days before the war ended. Others, however, still died after the war ended and four more would be added to the Memorial before it was unveiled in 1923. They were George Wright, Leonard Rose, Harry Hancock and Frank Davis. With the loss of 63 men, Bidford had paid a heavy price in the 'war to end all wars'. May they and the millions of others all rest in peace.

2/5th Battalion, Royal Warwickshire Regiment marching back from the trenches, Frevent, 8 April 1918.
(Photograph courtesy of Imperial War Museum - Q 329)

"We Will Remember Them"

Pte. C. R. PULHAM,
M.G.C.
(Killed.)

Cecil Raymond Pulham
Private 19934, 14th Battalion,
Machine Gun Corps (Infantry).
Died: Thursday 21st March 1918, aged 22.
Buried at Montescourt-Lizerolles, France.
Medals: 1914-15 Star, British and Victory medals.

Cecil Pulham was the son of William and Ellen Pulham (nee Phipps) of Falcon Buildings, Bidford. He had two brothers and four sisters and was born at Abbots Morton in Worcestershire. In 1911 the family had been living in Bleachfield Street, Alcester before moving to Bidford. His father was a farm labourer and Cecil, who was then fifteen, was working as a ploughboy.

Cecil was an early volunteer enlisting in the second week of September 1914 in Birmingham. He originally joined the King's Royal Rifle Corps as Rifleman no. A/1583. On completing his training, he was posted to France on 21st May 1915 where he became a member of the battalion's machine gun section. On the 24th February 1916 the 42nd Brigade Machine Gun Company was formed at Houtkerque. Part of this brigade was the 9th King's Royal Rifle Corps machine gun section. The 42nd were engaged in the Battle of the Somme 1916, taking part in action at Delville Wood, Flers-Courcelette and the German retreat to the Hindenberg Line in March/April 1917. He saw action at Arras during the first and third Battles of the Scarpe. He then moved to Belgium for the Battle of Ypres, seeing action at Langemarck, Menin Road and the first Battle of Passchendaele.

He returned home for his last leave in December 1917 but had to rejoin his unit the week before Christmas. On 21st March 1918 he was in the front line near to St

Quentin. This was the day the Germans launched the great Spring Offensive known as 'Operation Michael' or the 'Kaiserschlacht'. A few weeks later his mother received a letter from a comrade informing her of Cecil's death. He said that while in action during the retreat, Cecil had been shot in the thigh but had died while they were putting a dressing on the wound. Before Cecil's death his father and a brother-in-law had already been lost in the war. His grave is in the village cemetery at Montescourt-Lizerolles and one of his comrades is also buried there, Private 19965 T. E. Wooding, who came from London.

The author at the grave of Cecil Pulham

Alfred Henry Beard

Sergeant 31117, 2nd Battalion, Oxford and Bucks Light Infantry.
Died: Saturday 20th April 1918, aged 23.
Buried at Bac-du-Sud British Cemetery, France (plot 2, row B, grave 5).
Medals: British and Victory medals.

Alfred Beard was the youngest son of Henry and Elizabeth Beard (nee Collins) of Barton. He had three brothers and three sisters and was born in Stratford-upon-Avon. The 1911 census shows him living in Barton working as a farm labourer as was his father and an older brother John. He married Ethel M. Biddle in 1915 in Portsmouth. At the time they were living at Brockenhurst. By 1916 they had moved to Lymington and it was here, on 19th October 1916 that their only daughter, Floraline May, was born.

Alfred was an early recruit, enlisting in Birmingham in September 1914 with the 2nd Battalion the Oxford and Bucks Light Infantry. On completing his training he soon gained promotion, reaching the rank of Quartermaster-Sergeant. Most of his war service was spent in England training recruits but he was finally posted to France on 15th March 1918, just six days before the German Spring Offensive. He would have been at Vallubart Camp, Ypres on the 21st when the attack began. The battalion was part of the 3rd Army under the command of the Canadian General Byng. They were involved in the defence of St Quentin where the battalion suffered heavy losses. They were then involved in the Battle of the Lys (9th -29th April). On the 13th April Alfred celebrated his 23rd birthday and on 15th April he posted what was to be his last letter home. He said he was fine and there was no need for anyone to worry. Sadly, five days later he died from wounds received in action during the battle.

Following his death, Ethel re-married, becoming Mrs E. M. Collins. In 1946 Floraline married William A. Hawker in Southampton and she died there in 2006. Alfred's name also appears on the East Boldre War Memorial in Hampshire.

The Soldiers' Stories - 1918-1922

Alfred Beard with his wife, Ethel and daughter, Floraline May

"We Will Remember Them"

Francis Liddell
Private 28633, 1st Battalion, Hampshire Regiment.
Died: Monday 22nd April 1918, aged 19.
Commemorated on the Loos Memorial, France (panel 73).
Medals: British and Victory medals.

Francis Liddell was the second son of William and Annie Liddell (nee Albutt). He had been born at Clent in Worcestershire. His father was a game-keeper and Francis, like his late brother William, was a farm labourer.

Francis joined the army on 2nd March 1917, enlisting in Stratford-on-Avon. He went to Broadstairs for his basic training and was then sent to Ipswich. He was sent with the draft to France on 2nd April 1918 serving with the 1st Battalion the Hampshire Regiment; this was just 20 days before he was killed. His parents received information that he was missing in action following the German attack on 22nd April, during the Battle of the Lys and Bethune. The Germans called it 'Operation Georgette'. After reports had been gathered of the action, they received official confirmation on 13th June 1918 that Francis had indeed been killed on the 22nd and his body was never recovered. He was their second son to die as his elder brother William had been killed just five months before. Both are also remembered on the Welford on Avon war memorial as their Bickmarsh home was part of Welford's ecclesiastical parish during World War One.

Two Ways of "Helping to Win."

First— Buy National War Bonds.

Buy as many and as often as you can. The greater your purchases of National War Bonds, the greater the comfort of the armies fighting for you; the greater the power of the offensive; the sooner will come the battle which will force the Peace Terms that you want. You can purchase National War Bonds at any Money Order or Post Office from £5 upwards.

Second— Drink Coffee for Breakfast.

To alter your Breakfast "taste" for the time being is not a great sacrifice, but it will enable the Food Controller to more easily cope with the present shortage of Tea. You can purchase at the International

Delicious Pure Coffee 1/6 and 1/8

International Stores

THE BIGGEST GROCERS IN THE WORLD

TEA :: COFFEE :: GROCERIES :: PROVISIONS

I.S. 105.

450,000 More Men.

TO MEET THE COMING GERMAN OFFENSIVE.

HOW THEY ARE TO BE FOUND.

The important point in the speech of Sir Auckland Geddes in the Commons on Monday was the strength of the coming German offensive in the West and how the Allies are going to meet it.

According to the new Minister of National Service as the result of the Russian col-

England	4,530,000	60.4 per cent.
Scotland	620,000	8.3 "
Wales	280,000	3.7 "
Ireland	170,000	2.3 "
Dominions & Colonies	900,000	12.0 "

The remaining million men, composed of native fighting troops, labour corps, carriers, etc., represent the contribution made by India and our various African and other dependencies.

WHEN FOOD UPSETS YOU.

Food is as important to the sick person as medicine, more so in most cases. A badly chosen diet may retard recovery.

MINE EXPLOSION.

FEARED LOSS OF 160 LIVES IN STAFFORDSHIRE DISASTER.

DISTRESSING SCENES.

As a result of the terrible explosion which occurred at the Minnie Pit, Halmer End, near Hanley, it is feared that 160 miners have lost their lives. When the explosion occurred there were 247 men and youths in the workings, and up to Tuesday night 87 had been rescued (including 11 who had been gassed); 23 dead bodies had been recovered

"We Will Remember Them"

Thomas William Millward

Sapper 188908, Railway Operation Division, Royal Engineers.
Died: Monday 27th May 1918, aged 27.
Buried in Mendingham Military Cemetery, Proven, Belgium (plot 10, row D, grave 10).
Medals: British and Victory medals.

Thomas Millward was the son of Walter and Alice Annie Millward (nee Evans) and was born in Bewdley in Worcestershire. He had an older sister Annie and a brother George and as a lad attended Bewdley Grammar School. The census of 1911 shows him in lodgings at the home of Henry and Anne Barrell at 19 Stourbridge Road, Halesowen and he was employed as a railway clerk. He married his wife Sarah in 1913 and they had two children born in Halesowen. The family then moved to Salford Road, Bidford. Thomas was by then working as a booking clerk at Salford Priors Railway Station, employed by the Midland Regional Railway.

He enlisted as a Sapper in the Royal Engineers in Stratford-on-Avon on 23rd June 1916. On completing his training he was sent to France on 11th September 1916. He was to spend a lot of time at Rouen before being sent up to the Front. His unit was responsible for the operation and building of light railways up to the Front. They were used to carry

122

ammunition, supplies and troops to the line and to ferry the wounded back to hospitals. He last came home on leave on 1st December 1917 and on returning to his unit, was sent to the Ypres Salient in Belgium.

The next news of Thomas was when his wife received a letter from his company captain. He informed her that Thomas had been killed in action by enemy shellfire late in the evening on 27th May 1918 and had been buried the next day with full military honours. He expressed great sympathy and said that her husband was devoted to his duty and was a very dependable man. Mendingham Cemetery was the site of a casualty clearing station during the war.

Aerial view of Dernancourt showing the Albert–Amiens railway line and road leading under the railway bridge towards the Dernancourt Communal Cemetery, Dernancourt, France, May 1918.

A01058, Australian War Memorial

"We Will Remember Them"

Carl Rudolf Pitcher

Private 36422, 2nd Battalion, Wiltshire Regiment.
Died: Thursday 30th May 1918, aged 19.
Buried at Chambrecy British Cemetery,
France (plot 1, row A, grave 2).
Medals: British and Victory medals.

Carl Pitcher was the second son of Thomas William and Ruth Pitcher (nee Hope). He was born in Wellesbourne and had three brothers and one sister. Before the war the family were living in Falcon Buildings in Bidford, then moving to 70 Charlotte Road, Stirchley, Birmingham.

Carl joined the army in November 1917, enlisting in Birmingham. He joined the Wiltshire Regiment and was sent to Salisbury Plain for his basic training. He was drafted to France in April 1918 to help try and stem the German Spring Offensive which had begun on 21st March. He would have been involved in the Battle of the Lys (9th-29th April) and during this battle the battalion were in action at Bailleul (13th-15th April) at

Chambrecy British Cemetery. Photograph courtesy of Garitan

Kemmel (25th-26th April) and on the 29th at Scherpenberg. On 13th May the battalion became part of the 19th Western Division. Carl would have taken part in the Battle of the Aisne (25th May-7th June) and it was during this battle that he was killed. On the opening day of the attack the German General Ludendorff used 41 divisions against the 12 British divisions. In the opening barrage the Germans used six thousand guns and fired two million shells in four hours. Carl's parents received notification that their son was missing and wounded during the battle on the 30th April. They later received notification from the War Office that he had been killed that day.

"We Will Remember Them"

Philip Dance

Driver 130236/Private 143146, Royal Field Artillery /49th Agricultural Company Labour Corps.
Died: Friday 28th June 1918, aged 26.
Buried at Stow-on-the Wold Cemetery, Gloucestershire.
Medals: 1914-15 Star, British and Victory medals.

Philip Dance was the youngest son of William and Sarah Dance (nee Cottrell) of Marlcliff. The family lived in a farm-tied cottage belonging to the Langston family. His father worked as a carter on the farm and his mother was a dress-maker. The 1911 census also shows Philip as a farm worker. Following this, he went to work as a steam roller driver's assistant for Bomford and Evershed. He was next employed at Broom Mill by Adkins and Thomas where his job was delivering grain for horses. It was while delivering grain in Stow-on-the-Wold that he met his future wife, Annie Elizabeth Betteridge, who was the daughter of a farrier/shoesmith. Philip then went to work for her father as a groom and lived with the family in Camp Gardens. He married Annie on 21st May 1914 at the local Baptist chapel in Stow and afterwards they set up home in Chapel Street.

Philip enlisted in the army in March 1915 in Stratford-upon-Avon. He became a driver in the Royal Field Artillery and was posted to France. At some stage he was badly wounded while in France but it is not known exactly when. On recovering from his wounds, he was medically downgraded and transferred into a Labour Unit. On 21st February 1917, all Labour Units were brought together to form the Labour Corps. Philip was posted with the agricultural section to Taunton in Somerset where he worked on local farms. His wife, who at the

Stow-on-the-Wold War Memorial

Philip Dance outside his Stow home, possibly recently after enlistment.
Photograph courtesy of
M. Mumford collection

time was living with her parents in Stow, decided to move down to Manor Farm in Chedzoy so she could be near him.

While at work one day, he was kicked in the abdomen by a farm horse. The injuries he received caused inflammation of the peritoneum. He was taken to Bridgewater Hospital where he died on 28th June 1918. An inquest was held in Bridgewater on 1st July and proof of identity was given by his wife. The verdict was given as accidental death. His body was then taken back to Stow-on-the-Wold. He was buried with full military honours on Wednesday 3rd July 1918 and the service was conducted by the Reverend J. T. Evans. Besides his wife, he left two small children, Philip and William, the elder being just four years old. Annie re-married but by a strange twist of fate, her second husband was also to die after being kicked in the head by a horse.

"We Will Remember Them"

Reginald Russell
Private 23133, 16th (Service) Battalion,
Royal Warwickshire 3rd Birmingham Pals.
Died: Wednesday 21st August 1918, aged 20.
Buried at Adanac Military Cemetery, Miraumont and Pys, France (plot 3, row H, grave 19).
Medals: British and Victory medals.

Pte. R. RUSSELL, Royal Warwicks (Killed.)

Reginald Russell was the son of Walter Eli and Emma Elizabeth Russell (nee Davis). He was born in Bidford and the family lived on Tower Hill. Reginald was the youngest of the family, having three brothers and a sister. He also had a step-sister, Edith Morrall, and a step-brother, Herbert Davis, who had been killed in 1916. His civilian occupation is unknown.

Reginald joined the army in January 1917, enlisting in Birmingham with the 3rd Birmingham Pals. On completing his training, he was with the battalion during the third Battle of Ypres. In November 1917 the battalion was sent to take part in the Italian Campaign against the Austrians. In March 1918 they returned to France just in time for the massive German Spring Offensive.

Having halted the Germans at last, the British began the advance to victory in August 1918. On the morning of the 21st August 1918, Reginald, along with his battalion, attacked at 04.55 am, the objectives being Bocquoy and then a line just short of Achiet-le-Petit. By the end of the day the battalion had advanced fifteen miles in sixteen hours. Casualties at that time were quite light; one officer killed and five wounded and among other ranks 49 wounded and 11 killed – sadly, Reginald was one of those. Since arriving in Belgium in 1917 he had not been home on leave.

His mother received a letter from his company commander informing her of his death.

The Soldiers' Stories - 1918-1922

He went on to say that Reginald was one of his best men and that he was always cheerful and never afraid of work. He was much liked by both officers and men. His three elder brothers had all been discharged from the army on medical grounds. As a point of interest, Adanac (where he is buried) is Canada in reverse and the cemetery contains many Canadian graves.

"We Will Remember Them"

Christopher John Samuel Wilkes

Air Mechanic 2nd Class, 64043, Royal Air Force.
Died: Saturday 24th August 1918, aged 19.
Buried at Etaples Military Cemetery,
France (plot 67, row G, grave 27).
Medals: British and Victory medals.

Christopher Wilkes was the son of Christopher Ernest and Louisa Harriet Wilkes (nee Osborne). His birth is recorded as being in two different places; in 1901 it is shown as St John's, Worcestershire and in 1911 as Rushwick in Worcestershire. In 1901, the family were living at Broom Inn where his father was the publican. By 1911 they were living at Whitlinge in Worcestershire and his father was now a bailiff and market gardener. By the time of Christopher's death they had moved again and were living at Brookhouse in Salford Priors. Before the war Christopher was employed as a chauffeur for the Bishop of Worcester. He had two sisters, Annie and Nellie.

Christopher joined up in March 1917, joining what was then the Royal Flying Corps. On completion of his training, he was posted to Italy in December 1917, around Christmas time. He remained there until Easter 1918 when he was posted to France. On 1st April 1918 the Royal Flying Corps became the Royal Air Force. He was stationed at Etaples and was attached to the General Headquarters of the British Expeditionary Force.

He came home on leave at the beginning of August 1918 which was his first leave since joining up. He returned to France on 14th August, just ten days before his death. His parents received official notification that on 24th August he had suffered an attack of heart failure and had drowned in two feet of water while out bathing. One can imagine the shock and grief of his family who would have thought no harm would come to him where he was stationed. They received letters of condolence from the King and Queen and also from the Bishop of Worcester.

The Soldiers' Stories - 1918-1922

Sergt. F. WRIGHT,
Gloucesters
(Died of Wounds.)

Pte. J. TRACEY,
M.G.C.
(Military Medal.)

Lance-Corpl. H. G. SMITH
(Killed.)

Pte. W. R. WALDEN,
Royal Berks
(Accidentally Killed.)

Pte. R. H. DRURY,
Australian Forces
(Military Medal.)

Sergt. S. BEGLEY,
Royal Warwicks
(Killed.)

Lieut. CASTLE,
R.G.A.
(Killed.)

Air Mech. C. S. J. WILKES,
R.A.F.
(Accidentally Drowned.)

Sergt.-Major A. J. F. CLEMENTS,
Worcesters
(Killed.)

LOCAL WAR NOTES AND NEWS.

PORTRAITS.

Our first portrait this week is that of Pte. Martin C. March, of the Worcesters, son of Mr. and Mrs. Martin March, of Rynal-street, Evesham, and a former employe at the "Journal" Office, who was reported killed in July, 1917, and whose parents have just received the Military Medal awarded him for gallantry. The second is that of Pte. George Gale, of the Devons, son of Mr. and Mrs. W. the R.G.A., son of Mr. and Mrs. E. Castle, of Wyck Hill Lodge, Stow-on-the-Wold, who has been killed in action. The seventeenth is that of Air Mechanic Christopher S. J. Wilkes, of Salford Priors, who was accidentally drowned as reported last week. The last is that of Batt-Sergt.-Major A. J. F. Clements, of Ashton-under-Hill, who was reported missing in April last, and is now officially reported killed on that date.

HOW PTE. A. J. STREET DIED.

EVESHAM LAD DIES OF WO FRANCE.

Official intimation was recei day week that Able Seaman A Hawke Batt., 63rd (R.N.) Divi of wounds in France on Aug a son of Mr. and Mrs. A. Brotherton's-gardens, Little Evesham, and joined the N June, 1915, at the age of 17. to France three times and trench fever twice, and was t nital on both occasions in E September he was again broug suffering from severe gunshot arms, and returned to France la being home on leave for a sh field card was received from hi ago dated August 24, the day killed. The following letter w his mother on Monday last Dear Mrs. Hawker,—Although has already written you, I felt like to write also, for I was i the platoon your son was in, the time of his death. I mus deepest sympathy. I found hi good soldier and a good fellow. and steady always, and cheer the worst phases of warfare ar At the time of his death, I h a chosen band who set out t duty, which, however, was su formed. I conclude with very Yours sincerely, E. J. C. M several years Able Seaman H the employ of Mr. John B Abbey Gardens. His brother the present time in the Royal was first of all in the Royal rejected, afterwards joining t Regt., and he was in very d and was for a time a patient Sanatorium, subsequently joir Air Force.

EVESHAM LAD KILLED BY

Mr. and Mrs. R. H. Harri mon-road, Evesham, have rec tion that their son, Gnr. C Harris, of the Machine Gun C killed by a shell, which is ex following letter received l mother:—"3/9/18. Dear Mad probably heard that Gnr. C. your son, I presume—fell in ac 22. Accept my deepest sympat feel the blow only as those rest assured that he did his regret I cannot give you an but you will be able to obta unit. I happened to be in t with the Tanks and when I l saw him lying in a shell-hole took the enclosed from his p you would like to have then will receive them safely. A to express my sympathy in was probably killed by a sh vancing with his gun.—Yours D. J. Morgan, 2nd Lieut." ceived the contents of her son safely, consisting of pocket photos, etc., and was natura tressed on receiving them. G joined the Worcester Regt. October, and went out to Fr ing February at the age of 19. wards transferred to the Macl He was home on leave just be mas. For several years he wa of Mr. Fred Watkins, Eyesh time of joining the Army v the Evesham Saw Mills. His Harris, is in the Army and trench feet and fever when is at the present time at Be

SIGNALLER S. COURT KILL

Signaller Stanley Court, of t Borderers, of Rogerstone, Mon., has been killed in act He is a nephew of Mr. and M of Evesham, with whom hi Elsie Court, who is employed & H. Smith, Ltd., lives

ANOTHER OFFENHAM LAD

131

"We Will Remember Them"

Charles Heaver

Private CH/1676(S), Royal Marine Light Infantry,
1st Battalion Royal Naval Division.
Died: Sunday 25th August 1918, aged 39.
Buried at Valenciennes (St Roch)
Communal Cemetery,
British Extension, France (plot 5, row E, grave 27).
Medals: British and Victory medals.

Charles Heaver was the son of Resta and Ellen Heaver (nee Kember). He was born at Godstone in Surrey where his father was a grocer and draper's assistant. He had two brothers and two sisters and was the youngest in the family. In the census of 1911 he is shown lodging at the home of Job and Annie Lea in Bidford, which was Borris Cottage at the bottom of the High Street. He was a painter by trade. In late 1915 he married their eldest daughter, Gertrude Annie Lea, who was a music teacher. They lived at Borris Cottage and had one daughter, called Mona.

Charles enlisted in the Marines on 18th August 1916 aged 37 years and 9 months. He did his training at Deal and Blandford and embarked in the Royal Marine Brigade on 1st November 1916. He was sent to France on 10th April 1917 as part of the 1st Marine Battalion. On 2nd May 1917 he became Assistant Provost Marshal. On 15th October 1917 he re-joined his battalion.

In March 1918 he was in the front line when the Germans launched their Spring Offensive on the 21st. Gertrude received information at the end of April that Charles went missing in action on 23rd March 1918. Her next news was a card from him on 23rd June saying he was a prisoner of war. Sadly, she then heard that he had died of ill health on 25th August 1918 in the prisoner of war camp, due to its poor condition. Gertrude was notified in October 1922 that his grave had been discovered in

The Soldiers' Stories - 1918-1922

Picture: Mona Arrowsmith (nee Heaver)

Valenciennes Communal Cemetery and his remains had been exhumed and re-buried in the British extension. An inscription was put on the headstone which read: "We miss you and mourn you in sorrow unseen and live on the memories of the days that have been". It cost the family £1.8d to put the inscription on, which was 71 letters at three pence halfpenny per letter.

George James Oakey

Private 30290, 3rd Battalion, Grenadier Guards.
Died: Wednesday 20th September 1918, aged 28.
Buried at Hermies Hill British Cemetery,
France (plot 3, row B, grave 26).
Medals: 1914-15 Star, British and Victory medals.

George Oakey was the son of Charles and Mary Oakey (nee Ewers) and was born at Barn Cottage, Crowle on 8th September 1890. He had two sisters and one brother. Before the war he was living with his sister Louise at Barton House, Barton and at this time he was employed as a game-keeper by Mr George Henry Fosbroke.

He enlisted at Stratford-upon-Avon on 26th November 1914. His form was filled in by Sergeant Williams of the Royal Warwickshire Regiment. George was shown as being 5ft 9 inches tall with a chest measurement of 36 inches with a 2 inch expansion. He joined the 2nd Life Guards at Windsor on 30th November with the rank of trooper and the serial number 3558. Following basic training, he landed in France on 1st August 1915. He remained in France with the battalion until returning to England on 6th June 1916. Here he remained until returning to France on 8th November 1916. He had sailed from Southampton and had landed at Le Havre. He was appointed to the rank of Lance-Corporal in the field on 1st January 1917; this appointment was confirmed on 6th January. On 15th January 1917 he was admitted to hospital where he was treated for scabies which was rife in the trenches. On 13th March 1917 he was admitted to Number 6 Field Hospital as a result of a wound to his right knee. This he received while in the trenches near to the town of Arras. Three days later he was transferred to Number 7 Base Hospital at Le Treport which is situated on the French coast and he was then transferred back to England for treatment and to convalesce. He came home on leave for the last time in January 1918 and on the 29th of that month he was transferred into the Grenadier Guards. He was posted back to France on 31st March 1918 as a private and a

The Soldiers' Stories - 1918-1922

Lewis gun operator. On the same day he was made up to a lance-corporal unpaid. He had lost his rank prior to this when being transferred from the Life Guards to the Grenadiers. Ten days before arriving back in France, the Germans had launched their massive Spring Offensive and the allies, despite early retreats, finally held the line until the massive counter-attack commenced on 8th August 1918.

By September the Guards were advancing towards the Hindenburg Line, a German strong defensive position, part of which was the Canal du Nord. On 3rd September George lost his Lewis gun in action and on the 10th was reduced to the rank of private by his C.O. This was confirmed in orders on 14th September. On 20th September the Guards Brigade was ordered to attack east and west of the canal which at that time was dry and behind it were massive pill boxes with heavy machine guns located inside them. On 25th September a heavy German barrage descended on the battalion front and the Germans then attempted a raid on Number 4 Company. This was repulsed and the Germans had one man wounded but he managed to escape. Casualties from the German barrage were three killed and six wounded, one of those killed being George. His next of kin were notified of his death on 15th October 1918, nearly three weeks after it had happened.

Below: A section of George Oakey's service reords showing 1918, the year of his death

Gerald Gould

Private 36145, 10th Battalion,
the Royal Warwickshire Regiment.
Died: Friday 8th November 1918, aged 18.
Buried at Bettrichies Communal Cemetery,
France (row B, grave 2).
Medals: British and Victory medals.

Gerald was the son of Julia and the late John Gould of Tower Hill, Bidford. His father had been an agricultural labourer and he had five sisters and an elder brother called George.

He enlisted in February 1917 aged just 17 in Stratford-upon-Avon, joining the Oxford and Bucks Light Infantry. He was sent to Northumberland for his initial training and was then posted on service as Trooper H/57222 the Queen's Own Oxford Hussars to Dublin in southern Ireland. In June 1918 he was sent to France, having been transferred this time into the Warwicks. Following the allied attacks in August, the Germans were in full retreat by November and the war was nearly over. Even with peace talks going on, however, the Warwicks were ordered to continue the advance on 8th November and to attack east of Malplaquet. They were held up by German machine gun fire and Gerald was killed. The battalion suffered a total of three officers killed, five among other ranks and seven would die of wounds.

The following day at eleven o'clock, the battalion went into reserve and for them the war was over. Just 48 hours later, it was over for everyone.

Later in the month, just after the Armistice Day celebrations, Gerald's mother received a letter from his company commander informing her of Gerald's death on the 8th November. He said her son had been an excellent soldier and his loss was keenly felt by all the company. He went on to say that they all tendered their deepest sympathy to her.

Gerald Gould's grave - (photograph: Pierre Vandervelden, Peruwelz, Belgium)

He also informed her that Gerald had been buried the following Monday (Armistice Day) in a French cemetery along with two others from the battalion. One of these was Corporal Albert Steele who came from Alcester.

The killing, if not the dying, had ended.

"We Will Remember Them"

George Benjamin Wright

Private 16355, 8th (Service) Battalion (Pioneers),
Oxford and Bucks Light Infantry.
Died: Saturday 7th December 1918, aged 21,
Buried in Sophia War Cemetery,
Bulgaria (plot 3, row D, grave 4).
Medals: 1914-15 Star, British and Victory medals.

George was the son of Benjamin Wright and Alice (nee Hall) and was born at Harescombe in Gloucestershire. He had four brothers and two sisters. In 1911 the family were living at Wadboro Park in Worcester. George, then aged 14, was a farm labourer and his father was working as a waggoner. By 1914 the family had moved yet again to Barton and were living at New Cottages.

George enlisted in Birmingham in October 1914 in the Oxford and Bucks Light Infantry and the battalion was formed in Oxford. From there it went to Codford and was attached to the 26th Division. In November 1914 they went back to billets in Oxford and in March 1915 they became a Pioneer Battalion and were sent to Sutton Veny for training. In September 1915 they landed at Le Havre, France but the stay was short-lived. In November they moved to Marseilles and from there sailed to Salonika. It was here that George spent the rest of the war. The battalion would have been involved in trench-digging, wiring parties, road-making and repairing etc. Most of this would have been done under enemy fire.

At the end of the war George was stationed near the town of Strumica in Macedonia. Nine months earlier on 4th March 1918 Private Albert Gitchell, an American army cook at Fort Riley, Kansas, awoke with a temperature of 103. He was admitted to the infirmary with influenza. Within a month over 1,100 on the base in Kansas had gone down with it. Within a few months the Americans were in Europe and the Spanish 'Flu

The Soldiers' Stories - 1918-1922

"…Within a few months the Americans were in Europe and the Spanish Flu went on to claim nearly one 100 million victims by 1920."

went on to claim nearly 100 million victims by 1920. Having survived the hostilities, George sadly caught the flu and died with pneumonia, one of the awful side effects. George's other brother Fred had died in Gallipoli but another brother Charles, who was in the King's Shropshire Light Infantry, survived the war.

Leonard Sylvester Rose

Sapper 240134, Royal Engineers,
Railway Operating Division.
Died: 5th March 1919, aged 23.
Buried in St Laurence's churchyard, Bidford.
Medals: British and Victory medals.

Leonard Rose was born on 13th July 1896 and was the fourth son of Henry James and Sarah Ann Rose (nee Churchley) of the Blockhouses, Salford Road, Bidford. He had four brothers and one sister. Before the war he was working as a farm labourer as shown in the census of 1911, and then in 1915 he changed jobs and went to work for the Stratford Midland Junction Railway Company where he was employed as a porter.
He joined the army on 14th February 1917, enlisting in Stratford-upon-Avon. He was posted as a sapper to the Royal Engineers Railway Operating Division and following training was posted to France as a railway shunter. He did not, however, remain long in France as he was badly gassed and was discharged from the army as unfit on 24th July 1917. He had served for only five months.

On returning to Bidford, after a period of convalescence, he went to work as a market gardener's waggoner in the village. As with most cases of gassing, it led to his developing tuberculosis. He then caught the 'flu virus which swept the world from 1918 until 1920, known as the Spanish Flu. The combination of the two caused heart failure and Leonard died at home with his father by his side on 5th March 1919. His elder brother Arthur had died of wounds in 1915.

Following a military funeral, he was buried in St Laurence's churchyard on Saturday 8th March 1919. Many ex-servicemen attended the service and burial.

Pictured right, medal index card of Leonard Rose

The Soldiers' Stories - 1918-1922

"As with most cases of gassing, it led to him developing tuberculosis. He then caught the 'flu virus' which swept the world from 1918 until 1920, known as the Spanish Flu"

Harry Hancock

Private 24523, 11th Battalion,
Gloucestershire Regiment.
Date of death unknown, aged 22-25.
Place of burial unknown.
Medals: British and Victory medals.

Harry was born in 1896 in Newcastle-on-Tyne. His father, also called Harry, was a regular soldier serving in the King's Royal Rifle Corps. By the beginning of the Boer War, Harry's father had moved to Barton. After leaving school, Harry worked in domestic service.

He enlisted on 4th August 1915 at Chipping Campden and his age was shown as 19 years and ten days. He joined the 11th Gloucesters on 14th September at Belbus Park, having arrived there the previous day. He was under canvas from 13th to 20th September 1915 and then moved into hutments at Seaford. Some of these were in poor condition and owing to severe weather, Harry was subjected to exposure. He became very ill and because of this he was deemed to be unfit for military service and was discharged from the army on 16th December 1915.

He attended a medical board on 17th January 1917 and he stated that he was fairly well when he enlisted but subject to winter coughs. He became ill with stomach pains, sickness and a slight cough when at Seaford. He had been discharged on Form A7B204 for active tuberculosis of the left lung. His present weight was 6 stone 12 lbs while in health it was usually 9 stone 2 lbs. His Medical Board record (pictured opposite) show he had the following: "Hectse fever, temperature range of 97 to 103, a cough, night sweats, no haemoplysis, diarrhoea, vomiting and was clearly emaciated". Both lungs were, by then, showing advanced signs of TB. He was passed as totally disabled. Though not the cause, his time in the army had aggravated his condition.

The Soldiers' Stories - 1918-1922

At his Board Harry gave his occupation as domestic servant and his address as Clifford Chambers. Prior to this he had been in a sanatorium in East Anglia which was located in Colchester. His average weekly wage for six months up to August 1916 had been 16 shillings a week. He was awarded a pension of 20 shillings a week backdated to 15th November 1916. Where or when Harry died we cannot say as he is not shown in a parish magazine Roll of Honour in June 1918, so it must be assumed that his death occurred between then and 1922.

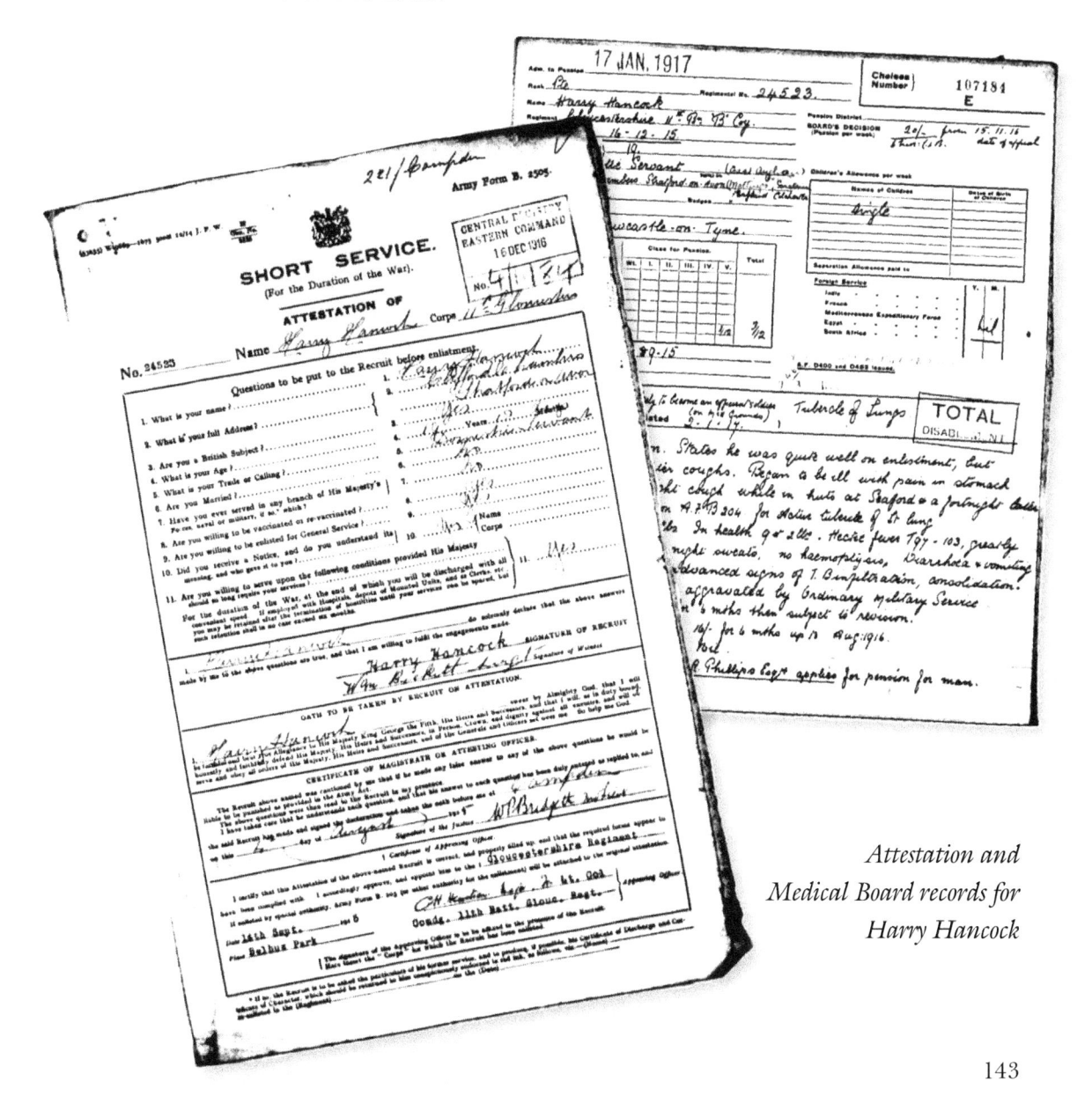

Attestation and Medical Board records for Harry Hancock

"We Will Remember Them"

IN MEMORY OF
THE MEN OF THIS PARISH
WHO GAVE THEIR LIVES IN THE GREAT WAR
1914 - 1919
AND TO COMMEMORATE VICTORY.

ASH, E.	HARTLAND, A.	PULHAM, C.
BEARD, A. H.	HARTWELL, H. F.	REEVES, N.
BENNETT, F. M.	HEAVER, C.	ROSE, A.
BENNETT, W. R.	HOUGHTON, B.	ROSE, L.
BLACKWELL, S. F.	HUGHES, R. G.	RICHARDSON, T. A.
CHURCHLEY, S.	LANE, W. G.	RUSSELL, T. A.
CLARKE, W.	LEONARD, G.	RUSSELL, R.
COLLETT, A.	LIDDELL, W.	SEYMOUR, J.
DANCE, P.	LIDDELL, F.	SHEASBY, E.
DAVIS, F.	LOCKE, N.	SMITH, J. C.
DAVIS, H.	McQUAY, F.	SMITH, F. G.
DEE, F. G.	MAYRICK, T.	STANFORD, L.
EDKINS, C. J.	MILLWARD, T. W.	TARRANT, F.
FREER, L. H.	MUMFORD, W.	TAYLOR, T.
FREEMAN, H.	NICHOLLS, H. A.	TAYLOR, W.
GARDNER, D.	OAKEY, G.	WHEATLEY, H.
GOULD, G.	PAYNE, W. J. H.	WILKES, C. J. S.
HANCOCK, F.	PITCHER, B. H.	WOODHOUSE, W.
HANCOCK, H.	PITCHER, C. R.	WRIGHT, F.
HARRIS, F.	POWER, C. H. F.	WRIGHT, G.
	PULHAM, W. F.	

144

Frank Davis

**Regiment unknown. Died: Wednesday 17th May 1922, aged 30.
Buried in St Laurence's churchyard, Bidford in an unmarked grave.
Medals: British and Victory medals.**

Frank was born at Salford Priors and was the son of Edwin and Annie Davis (nee Peats), his father was a bricklayer.

No records of Frank's military service survive and though there are medal index cards with either F or Frank Davis on them it would not be fair to assume which is his.

What is known, however, is that at some time during the war he had been gassed and because of this had been invalided out of the army with a disability pension. Before this had occurred, he had been living in Broom in 1916 with his wife Fanny. During this time Fanny gave birth to a son called Reginald. On Frank's return from the army the family moved from Broom into a small cottage in Icknield Street in Bidford. Frank then went to work as a farm labourer for Mr Fred Holder.

Many soldiers who had been gassed developed tuberculosis and Frank was no exception. He died at the cottage after a long and painful illness with his wife by his side. Sadly, soon after, his wife and son also contracted the disease and both died.

The memorial screen in St Laurence's church was erected before his death and therefore his name had to be added to the bottom, but his name does appear in the correct position on the War Memorial as this was not unveiled until 1923, so Frank's death brought a close to the Great War of 1914-18 for Bidford.

'May the Light of Heaven surround them'
(from an Irish War Memorial)

"We Will Remember Them"

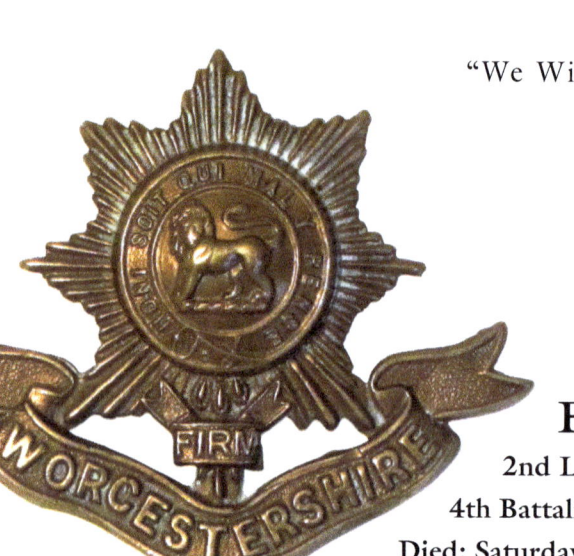

Edward Round

2nd Lieutenant,
4th Battalion, Worcestershire Regiment.
Died: Saturday 21st April 1917 aged 36.
Buried: Feuchy Chapel, British Cemetery Wancourt, Arras, (plot 1, row B, grave 43) and with a commemorative bench on Marriage Hill, Bidford-on-Avon.
Medals: British and Victory medals.

Although having no connection with Bidford through birth, marriage or residency, Edward enjoyed coming to Bidford and after his death, a seat with a commemorative plaque was placed on Marriage Hill, giving a lovely view over the village. It is because of this that a short note in his memory has been included.

Edward was born at 87 Hall Street in Dudley which was the site of the Plough and Harrow pub. He was the second son of Edmund and Sarah Round and was born in 1881. His father was a quarry labourer. His father and elder brother Joseph were by then railway labourers. A third son, Ernest, was born in 1885. By 1901 the family had moved again to 122 High Street, Dudley. His brother Joseph was by then working as an electrical mechanic. At this time, Edward and Ernest were employed

Photograph: Mick McCann, British War Graves

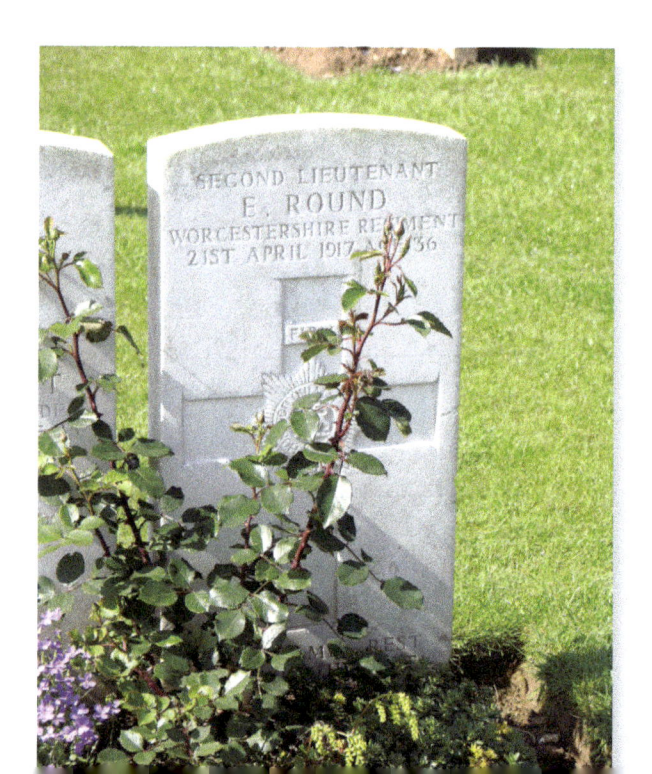

The Soldiers' Stories - 1918-1922

*Commemorative bench,
Marriage Hill,
Bidford-on-Avon*
Photographer: Sandra Parker

as draper's assistants. In 1905 he married Gertrude Lucy Field and in 1911 he was working as a woollen draper's assistant. Their home was at 46 Blackacre Road, Dudley. By the outbreak of war he was employed by the firm of Grainger and Smith Limited of High Street Dudley.

He enlisted in the Worcestershire Regiment during the war, joining the 4th Battalion. This would have been sometime during 1916 and his army number was 2936. He remained in England throughout 1916 and so missed the battalion's involvement on the Somme and Ypres Salient. He reached the rank of Company Quartermaster Sergeant before being promoted to the rank of temporary 2nd Lieutenant.

In 1917 he was posted to France, entering the theatre of war on 28th February. As part of the 29th Division, the battalion took part in the Battle of Arras. This began on 9th April with a successful Canadian attack on Vimy Ridge. It also became known as the first, second and third battles of the Scarpe. It was during the period between the first and second battles that Edward was killed in action on 21st April 1917. He had only been in France a total of 52 days. His widow received his medals in March 1922 and was by then living at 47 King Street Dudley.

147

Bidford and the First World War

"Keep the Home Fires Burning"

As families waited for news of their loved ones, the people of Bidford were anxious to feel that they were 'doing their bit' to help with the war effort and fund-raising was a popular way of doing this. By December 1914: "the third smoking concert of the war was held at the Fisherman's Rest Pub (now an optician's and hairdresser's premises)…to raise funds for the troops"[11].

Fund-raising was to continue in various forms throughout the war, as in 1916 when "a day of patriotic billiards was played at the White Lion Hotel (now apartments) between Mr W. Smith, a Coventry professional and Mr G. Owen, the ex-amateur champion from Sheffield. This was in aid of the Sportsman's Ambulance Fund. Various sports including cricket, football, rugby, darts etc are involved, £40,000 being the target and half already is raised. Several ambulances have been presented to the Colours."[12] Even the village children contributed and a teacher recorded in the school log-book in May 1915 that: "I suggested that the children should bring their coppers (pennies) to school to buy materials for sandbags as they are being made by helpers in the village. The children were delighted to help and today Miss Fosbroke, the organiser of the "Sand bag Party", visited the school and received three shillings and eight pence halfpenny from the little ones".

11. *Evesham Journal, 5th December 1914*

12. *Evesham Journal, 11th October, 1914*

Collecting for the Voluntary Aid Detachment by Bidford Bridge
Photograph courtesy of the Rodney Crompton collection

The village school continued to help with the war effort as in March 1916 they had an "Egg Day" when they brought in eggs for wounded soldiers. 260 eggs were collected and sent to Clopton Military Hospital in Stratford-upon-Avon, followed by pots of potatoes later in the month. In October 1916 the children were visited by one of the soldiers from the village who was home on leave. Tom Smith, a former pupil, brought a German rifle bayonet and a gas mask for the children to inspect. "Very great interest was shown in these articles, many children putting on the gas mask" noted the School logbook.

The children must have had the effects of the war brought home to them as the school records show that in November 1914 three Belgian refugee children were admitted to the school; two boys and a girl, the boys being named as Henri and Jacques Scham. Belgian refugees had come to the village as a result of the war, nine of whom were members of the Bidford-on-Avon Rifle and Drill Association. In December 1914 a War Refugee Meeting was held in the old schoolroom. There were 15 Belgian refugees in Bidford, whom they were:

"entertaining to the best of their ability with due regard to strict economy. They have two cottages generously placed at their disposal and they have two committees of ladies, one for each household. Response to appeal for subscriptions had been both general and generous and many had contributed in kind. Although they had money at hand, further help was needed...Some of the refugees were working and the committee allowed them one-fourth of their earnings for themselves, the other went to the fund."[13]

December also saw the first Christmas of the war and being a rural area was a decided advantage regarding access to food:

"The butchers are arranging a good show. Mr Winnett has some prime meat including two heifers from the Manor Farm, Cleeve Prior, one from Broom Court, one from Bidford Grange and one from Hillborough Manor, and some fine legs from Bickmarsh Hall Estate. Also Mr Wilkes' establishment has some choice heifers and prime mutton from the Christmas sales at Stratford-upon-Avon and Alcester. Mr Prickett has some fine carcasses of beef, including a fat bullock from the Stratford Christmas sale and a prime heifer from the Alcester Christmas market. He has also some prime leg mutton."[14]

Recruitment march through Bidford
Photograph courtesy of the Rodney Crompton collection

---

13. Evesham Journal, 5th December 1914 • 14. Evesham Journal, 19th December 1914

As the war progressed, civilians became more directly affected and by 1916 air raids had become a reality of war. Although Bidford was too far inland to be in danger, the fear of air raids led the Bidford Gas Company (based in what is now Gashouse Lane) to issue a warning in February 1916 that:

"It may be necessary to turn off the gas in the event of an air-raid when householders should turn off meters and taps as failure to do so could lead to disastrous consequences."[15]

In a rural community, the production of food was a major occupation and was to increase in importance from 1916. The Bidford Pig Club continued to meet as many villagers owned their own pig and by the end of the year food production was being taken even more seriously since the Germans began their U-boat campaign to sink British shipping in an attempt to starve Britain into submission. In order to maximise food production, in April 1917 it was decided to form a Rat and Sparrow Club in Bidford: *"as a way of destroying these pests. The payment for these vermin killed would be....heads of sparrows 3d a dozen, eggs of sparrows 2d a dozen, tails of rats 3d each.*

For "our boys", Bidford 1917 - a fundraising event on Bank Square
Photograph courtesy of the Rodney Crompton collection

15. Evesham Journal, 12th February, 1916

Membership is to be an annual subscription for agriculturalists of 2/ 6d for 50 acres and working members 1/- a year."[16]

Harvesting produce meant that, with so many men away in the armed forces, as many people as possible were required to help. On 20th August 1915, the school log book recorded that: *"Recently our attendance has been very thin as so many boys have been needed for agricultural purposes, labour being very short. Plum picking is now in full swing, demanding the assistance of every available boy and girl"*. In June 1916 again, attendance was: *"…very poor…many of the children are now engaged in picking peas"* and in 1917 the teacher wrote that: *"I received notice on Sunday 30th September that the school was to be closed for a week as there was urgent need for the children to go potato picking"*.
Other areas of village life were feeling the effects of the menfolk's absence. In 1917, the Parish Council recorded that: *"Owing to the fact that several members of the Fire Brigade, including the captain, Mr F. Houghton, had been called up for military service, it was necessary to re-organise the brigade. The remaining three members…reported that they had obtained the consent of six men willing to join them for the period of the war"*.[17]

By 1918 not only food but petrol was rationed with the introduction of the Petrol Restriction Order. In May 1918, Arthur Tedd of Springbank, Bidford-on-Avon, appeared at the King's Heath Branch Court charged with using unauthorised petrol and also: *"driving a motorcycle and sidecar at a speed dangerous to the public on the Alcester Road, coming round a bend at 20 mph (the speed limit was 5 mph) and hitting "the left of a tramcar and scattering in all directions passengers who were alighting, including wounded soldiers."*[18]

In December 1918, Thomas Hugh Bird of Aston, Birmingham, was charged with: *"using petrol or a substitute for driving a motor car at Wixford on 9th December…a witness had stopped him and asked him on what business he was using the car…he explained that he was taking his wife to Bidford to stay for a few days for the sake of her health…he thought he could use the motor spirit under Clause III of the Petrol Restriction Order"*.[19]

Despite the grim news of casualties that the village had to bear, there was pride too. In 1917 they read in the Evesham Journal that: *"The Military Medal has been awarded to Lance-Corporal Jesse Moore of the Dorset Regiment for covering his company with machine*

---

16. Evesham Journal, 21st April, 1917 • 17. Evesham Journal, 13th March, 1917
18. Evesham Journal, 19th May, 1918 • 19. Evesham Journal, December, 1918

gun fire during an attack...he accounted for many Germans...The son of Mr and Mrs George Moore of Victoria Road, Bidford.....a member of the parish church choir......He joined the army in August 1914, being one of the first to volunteer from this parish. He has been in France nearly two years and has been in much of the fighting". [20]

As the war dragged on, the fund-raising continued. In January 1917: "members of the Girls' Friendly Society provided an enjoyable programme in the Old School Room for the Tobacco and Wool Funds which raise £4.10/-. *"The songs sung indicated the longing for the end of the conflict: 'When the War is Over, Mother Dear', 'It's a Long, Long Trail', 'When You Come Home' and 'Dreaming of Homeland'.*[21]

Fund-raising reached its peak in August 1918 during War Weapons Week. The Evesham Journal reported that: *"An open air meeting was held on Sunday evening on the bank in support of the War Weapon Week (August 11th-17th). The parish of Bidford is asked to invest £4,000 for the purchase of four guns. It was announced on Sunday that the cost of the first gun has already been promised... The Revd. J. W. Evans moved a resolution pledging the meeting to do all in their power to exceed the sum named as their goal. The resolution was carried by acclamation..."* By the end of the week: *"£4,000 was asked for to buy four guns, over £10,000 was invested. This sum represents over £450,000 today. This was the result of the efforts of the War Savings Committee here during the week. The committee was a thoroughly representative one and took up the work of canvassing in a business-like manner...Concerts were held on Thursday evening and Saturday evening on the Pleasure Grounds, kindly lent by Mr W. M. Holland...Friday was the children's day, the scholars from each school marched in procession from their schools to the War Savings Office (under the Assembly Rooms) and made their investments. All the children - except the infants who had their treat on the following Thursday – then proceeded to Holland's Pleasure Grounds where an excellent tea was provided and greatly enjoyed. Trips on the steamers on the Avon then followed, then games were entered into with zest and many good prizes competed for. Each child was given sixpence and a like amount was placed to their credit in the War Savings Association. These young folks had a most enjoyable time, thanks to the generosity of Mr Sam Mason and other friends. Saturday was indeed a busy day at the office with investments, the final figure raised being £10,584."*[22] This was a remarkable achievement for a village of about 1,500 and their support was finally rewarded at the end of the year.

20. Evesham Journal, 2nd June, 1917 • 21. Evesham Journal, January, 1917

22. Evesham Journal, 10th August 1918

" 'Bidford Gun Week' : Bidford school children line up outside the Assembly Rooms (now the site of The Bridge restaurant) to donate a penny"
Photograph courtesy of Molly Henderson collection

"We Will Remember Them"

Street parties on Church Street
Photograph courtesy of the Rodney Crompton collection

Organisers and caterers for the parties on Church Street. Bottom picture. Lady middle right in white is mother of Molly Henderson.
Photograph courtesy of Molly Henderson collection

The Armistice

The signing of the Armistice on 11th November 1918 brought relief and also wild rejoicing throughout the country, including in Bidford. The Evesham Journal reported on the reaction.

"Upon receipt of the splendid news there was an outburst of enthusiasm and in a very short time flags of almost all sizes and designs were flying from homes. Work ceased and everyone seemed bent on celebrating the joyful event. At 8 o'clock in the evening a huge bonfire was lighted on Tower Hill in the presence of a large assembly who sang and cheered themselves hoarse as they watched the flames. Quite a number of houses were illuminated and the bells pealed forth merrily from the church tower. On Monday and Tuesday there was foot racing in the main street".[23]

However, Bidford did not restrict its celebrations to 11th November. The following week the Journal reported from Bidford in its Saturday 23rd November edition that:

"Further joyous celebrations were held here on Friday night. A procession took place in which the Fire Brigade took part, upon the engine being placed an effigy of the Kaiser. The enthusiastic crowd which joined up were headed by the "Jamite Band" from the Broom Jam Factory... After the procession, the Kaiser was burnt on a bonfire on the island below the bridge, amidst loud cheers and a display of fireworks, generously supplied by Mr Sam Mason of Bell Court. The Pleasure Boat Inn (now The Frog pub) and several other residences were prettily illuminated the same evening. The scenes were witnessed by a large crowd. After the bonfire and display of fireworks a large number adjourned to the Fisherman's Rest where a smoking concert was held… .a number of patriotic speeches were delivered and there was much enthusiasm. Thanksgiving for the Cessation of Hostilities were held throughout the day at St Laurence's and St Matthew's, Broom."[24]

23. Evesham Journal, 16th November, 1918
24. Evesham Journal, 23rd November, 1918

Conclusion

So on the eleventh hour of the eleventh day of the eleventh month of 1918, four years and 90 days after it began, the Great War came to an end. Despite the rejoicing, there was, in reality, little to celebrate. Millions of soldiers and civilians had been killed and injured, empires had been destroyed and the Europe of the 19th century had disappeared. The war brought financial ruin to many countries; Britain was bankrupt by 1918 with costs of £745 billion pounds in modern terms. Large areas of northern France and Belgium were in ruins and would take years and huge costs to rebuild. The colossal numbers of French dead partly explain why the country was unable to resist the German invasion of 1940. The weakened financial state of Europe after the war eventually contributed to the Great Depression of the 1930s and the problems this caused in Germany were to lead to the rise of Adolf Hitler and the Nazi Party.

In Britain the war brought about the beginning of the breakdown of the Victorian way of life; women had been given the chance to work and have more freedom, the big houses and estates began to decline as many of the heirs had been killed and the expense of running them was no longer sustainable. Perhaps most of all, the war had a major impact on the populations in all those countries which took part in it.

Bidford mirrored thousands of villages throughout the land where the loss of so many young men was to be sorely felt. In Bidford there were 18 widows and 45 men who would never come back to marry village girls and provide a new generation. In a village of around 1,500, this was a considerable number and was to have a profound and lasting impact.

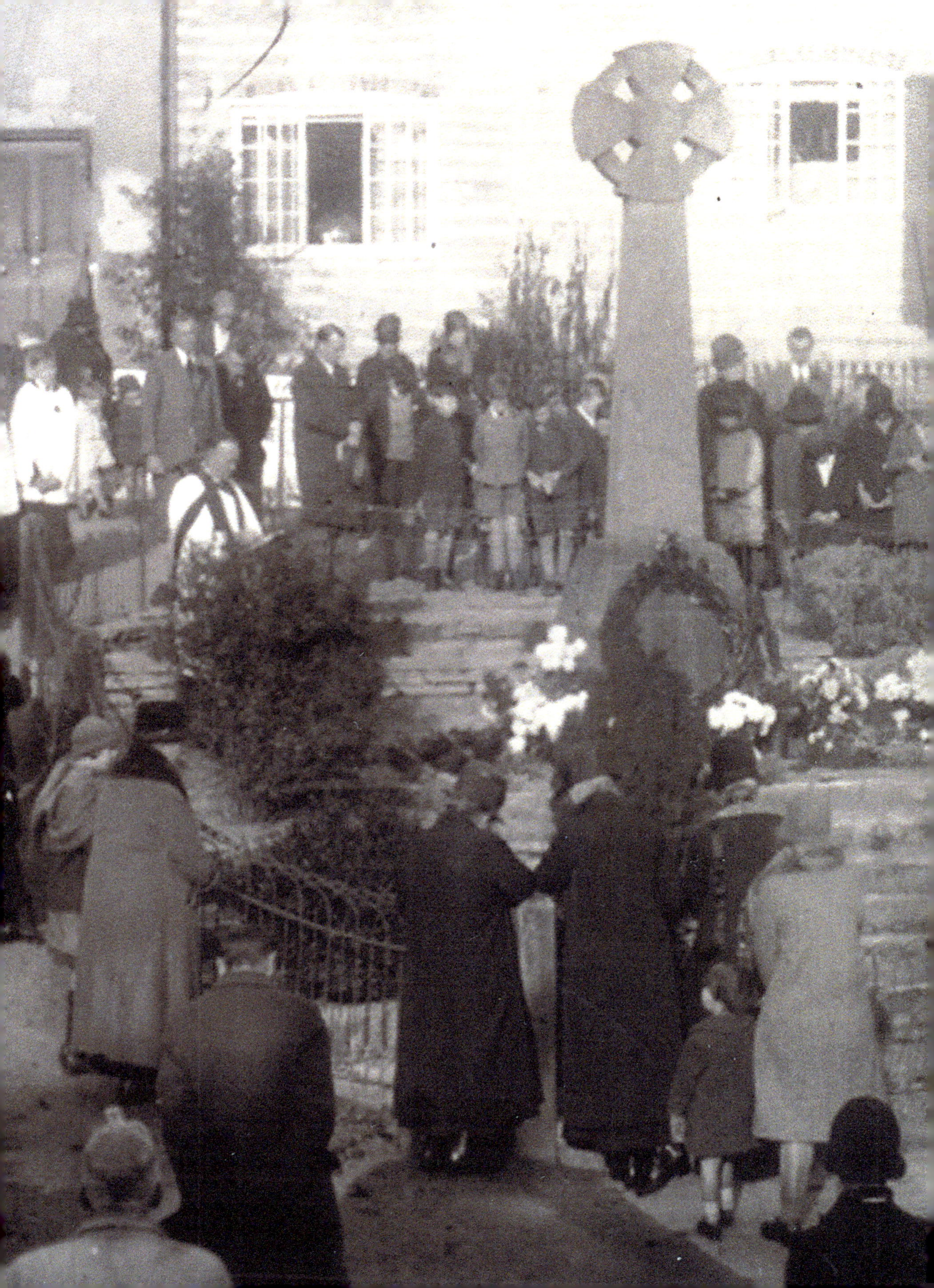

"We Will Remember Them"

On 29th April 1923, "In the presence of a very large assembly, the Memorial to the men of Bidford who gave their lives for their country in the Great War was unveiled and dedicated on Sunday evening. …The memorial was designed by…Mr G. F. Boshier …and suggested and erected by Mr W. H. Davis, monumental sculptor of Bidford. At 5.30, a good number of the ex-servicemen of the parish paraded near the Bridge and under command of Major G. F. Boshier, marched up the High Street to "the bank" on which the Memorial is erected. The unveiling ceremony was performed by Private Henry (Paddy) Locke, at the request of his comrades. Paddy belonged to the Sherwood Foresters[25] and went out with the first contingent of the Old Contemptibles and served at Mons. He was in France almost all through the war. …The vicar, the Revd. J. W. Evans, then dedicated the Memorial and the buglers sounded the "Last Post" followed by "Reveille". The hymn, 'O God our Help in Ages Past' was then sung, the singing led by the choir, and the vicar pronounced the Benediction. Mr J. D. Lane…then said a few words on behalf of the committee who had been able to bring about that solid recognition of the services of Bidford men who had helped attain victory and save the Empire. …He would appeal to them all, especially to the children, to reverence the Memorial and enclosure and to do all they could to see that it was not injured. …On behalf of the committee, he made over the Memorial to the Bidford people and trusted the Parish Council would see that every care was taken of it. …Dr Crawford accepted the Memorial on behalf of the Parish Council… with grateful thanks".[26]

Sadly, in less than 20 years' time, a new generation's names would be added to the Memorial to join those who had fought in 'the war to end all wars'.

---

25. *It should be noted that during the Great War Private Henry Locke served in the Royal Warwickshire Regiment.*
26. *Evesham Journal, 5th May, 1923.*

Conclusion

The unveiling of the Bidford-on-Avon War Memorial, 29th April 1923
Photograph courtesy of the Rodney Crompton collection

Here dead lie we because we did not choose

To live and shame the land from which we sprung.

Life, to be sure, is nothing much to lose;

But young men think it is, and we were young.

A. E. Housman

"We Will Remember Them"

Known Bidford Survivors

At the time of going to print it has been possible to identify many survivors of the Great War with Bidford connections. A project to investigate these and other possible survivors is underway and it is hoped that we can produce another publication telling their stories in due course. Already many interesting stories and photographs from relations have come to light. If you have any information regarding the following list of survivors or others not listed please contact the authors or Bidford & District History Society. We will endeavour to conduct further research on any connections provided at no charge.

Name	Regiment
Allen Reuben	Tank Corps
Bacon Arthur George	Army Service Corps
Bates F	Royal Warwickshire, Birmingham City Battalion
Beard George Ralf	Worcestershire
Beard William Maurice	10th Gloucestershire
Bennett Frederick William	Royal Warwickshire
Bennett Horace	Royal Garrison Artillery
Birchley Frederick	Warwickshire Yeomanry
Boshier Gilbert Arthur	Army Service Corps
Bott William	Oxford & Bucks Light Infantry
Bourne Edward	
Bradley Lawrence Reginald	Warwickshire Yeomanry
Bryan Percival	Royal Naval Air Service
Bryan Samuel	Worcestershire
Bubb George	Tank Corps
Coates John David	
Collett James	Royal Field Artillery
Cowper Raymond	Warwickshire Yeomanry
Cowper Wilfred	
Crompton George	Cheshires
Dance Charles	Royal Warwickshire
Dance Walter	Durham Light Infantry
Davis Henry Charles	Warwickshire Yeomanry

"We Will Remember Them"

Davis Charles Henry	Warwickshire Yeomanry
Elsmore James Harman	Royal Warwickshire
Faire Sydney George	Sherwood Foresters
Freeman George Henry	Royal Army Service Corps
Fryer John Frank	Royal Army Service Corps
Gardner L	4th Dragoon Guards
Goddard Ernest John	Royal Garrison Artillery
Gould Albert Victor	Warwickshire Yeomanry
Gould George Henry	Royal Garrison Artillery
Green H E	Machine Gun Corps
Harris B.H.H.	Oxford & Bucks Light Infantry
Harris Thomas	Coldstream Guards
Hartwell Harold James	Essex Regiment
Hartwell Walter Howard	Devonshire Regiment
Harwood Christopher	Gloucestershires
Harvey Malvern John	Gloucestershires
Harvey Thomas Stibbs	Gold Coast Defence Force
Haywood Charles	Royal Flying Corps
Hicks M	Worcestershire
Higley Albert	Lifeguards
Horseman Albert John	Lifeguards
Horseman Edward Victor	Royal Warwickshire
Houghton Capt. E	Royal Army Medical Corps
Houghton William	63rd Royal Naval Division
Houghton Frederick	
Jones G	Coldstream Guards
Kendall Harold	Army Service Corps
Locke George	Army Service Corps
Locke Henry	Royal Warwickshire
Locke William	Army Service Corps
Mason Richard	Warwickshire Yeomanry
Mayrick Alfred George	Royal Garrison Artillery
Mayrick James	Oxford & Bucks Light Infantry
Moore J	4th Dragoon Guards

Known Bidford Survivors

Moore Jesse Hunt	Dorset
Mundy Len	
Nicholls Sidney John E	
Nicholls S	Grenadier Guards
Nutting Owen John	Royal Field Artillery
Nutting Philip	Loyal North Lancs
Oliver William	Royal Naval Division
Osbourne Edward	Lincolnshire
Owen P.R.	Oxford & Bucks Light Infantry
Paddock William	Warwickshire Yeomanry
Payne Ernest Albert	Oxford & Bucks Light Infantry
Payne Percy	Duke of Cornwalls Light Infantry
Pritchard Eric	Devonshire
Pulham Edgar	Royal Navy
Pulham Francis	
Russell George Edwin	
Russell Victor Walter	
Russell William Albert	Royal Warwickshire
Sale George	Royal Field Artillary
Salisbury Frederick	Gloucestershire
Smith E S	
Smith Henry H	Warwickshire Yeomanry
Smith Thomas	Royal Warwickshire
Stanford W S	
Trayford George B	King's Liverpool Reg.
Tucker Howard	Machine Gun Corps
Vale Joseph	Royal Artillary
Vincent George	Royal Field Artillery
Wilcox G	
Wilkes Henry John	Oxford & Bucks Light Infantry
Wilkes Walter William	Royal Field Artillery
Wright Charles	King's Shropshire Light Infantry
Wright Robert William	Royal Warwickshire
Wyatt William Thomas	Royal Horse Artillery

"We Will Remember Them"

Statistics of the Fallen

The war had called together many men from different backgrounds and social classes, men of different ages and marital status. The typical soldier from Bidford would – perhaps consistent with one's pre-assumptions – have been single (70%), in his twenties (62%), worked in agriculture or associated trades (49%), served in one of the four local county regiments (43%), joined as and remained a private (76%) and been killed in action (57 %.) However, behind this stereotype, lies a more diverse range than one might have expected as the following statistics illustrate.

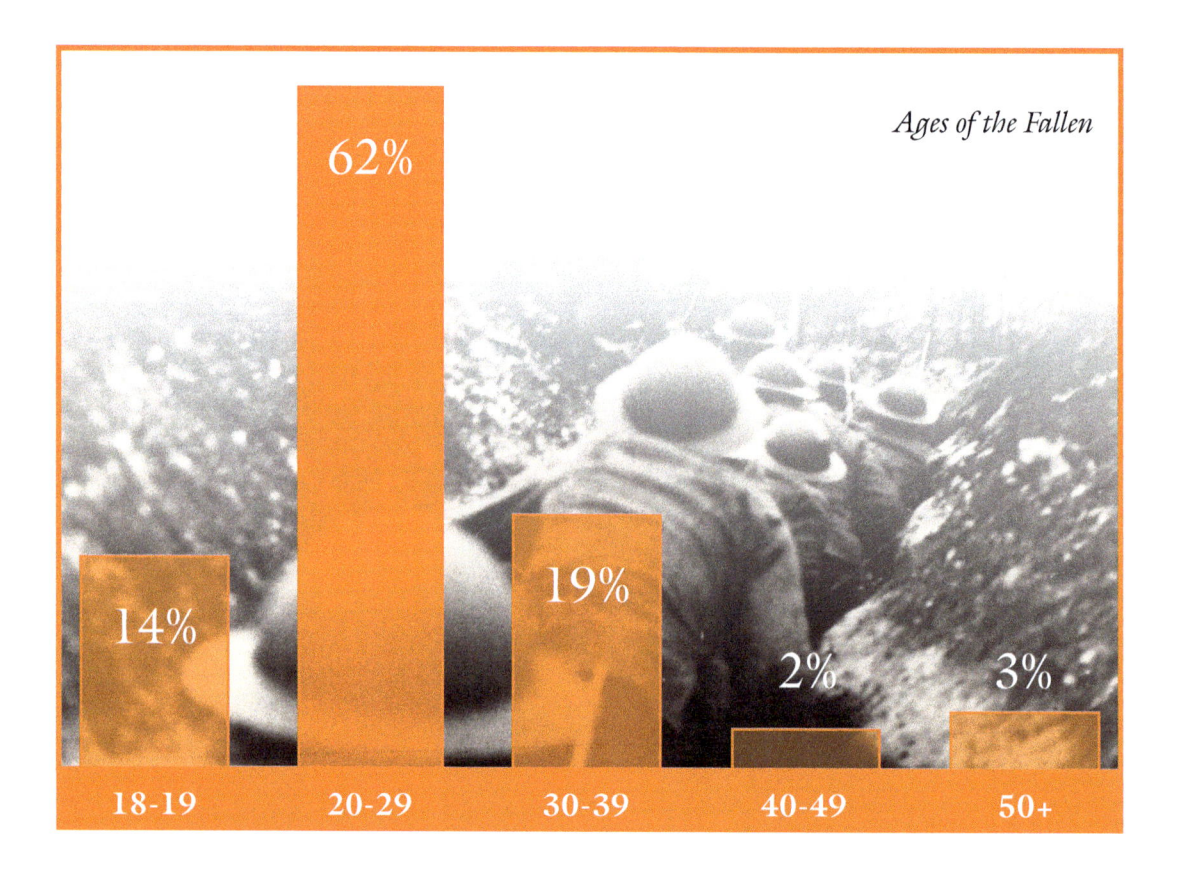

Ages of the Fallen

18-19	20-29	30-39	40-49	50+
14%	62%	19%	2%	3%

Statistics of the Fallen

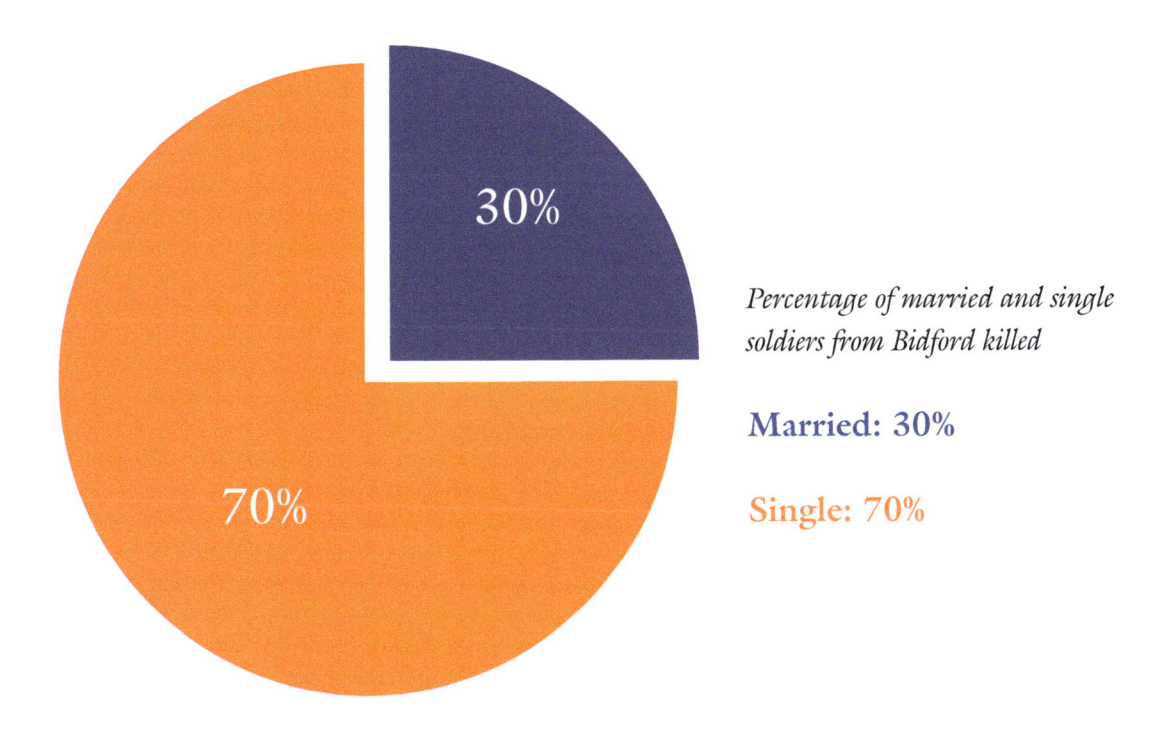

Percentage of married and single soldiers from Bidford killed

Married: 30%

Single: 70%

Employment

University	1	River dredger	1
Police	1	Regular army	3
Carpenter	1	Factory work	3
Railways	2	Grocery shop	1
Agricultural	29	Trainee manager	1
Chauffeur	1	Baker	1
Building	4	Lineman	1
Post Office	1	Cadbury's factory	1
Pub worker	1	Miller	1
Painter	2	Army pensioner	1
Steamroller driver	1	Farrier	1
Game-keeper	1	Domestic servant	3

Regiment

With one man's regiment unknown, it is surprising that 26 different regiments or units contained the fallen of Bidford though it could have been 27 as Captain Blackwell was shown in two at the time of his death.

Royal Warwickshire Regiment	9	Worcestershire Regiment	9
Oxford & Bucks Light Infantry	7	Royal Engineers	4
King's Royal Rifle Corps	3	Hampshire Regiment	3
Machine Gun Corps (Infantry)	2	Royal Field Artillery	2
Royal Army Service Corps	2	Wiltshire Regiment	2
Royal Garrison Artillery	2	Gloucestershire Regiment	2
Canadian Expeditionary Force	2	Grenadier Guards	1
Royal Flying Corps	1	Royal Air Force	1
Royal Marine Light Infantry	1	Royal Berkshire Regiment	1
South Staffordshire Regiment	1	King's Hussars	1
Essex Regiment	1	Dorset Regiment	1
Norfolk Regiment/Tank Regiment	1	Middlesex Regiment	1
Lincolnshire Regiment	1	Coldstream Guards	1
Unknown	1		

It should be noted that some of the men had also served in other regiments but for the purposes of this analysis, only their regiment at the time of death has been included.

Rank

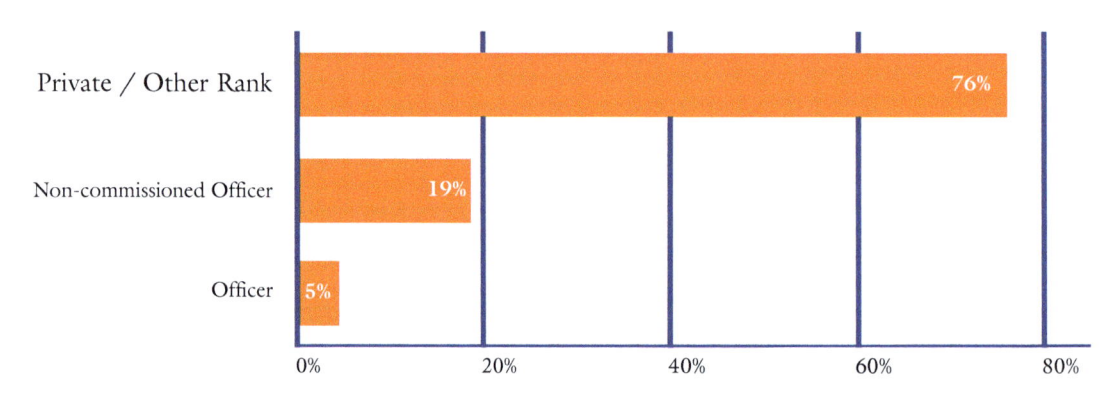

- Private / Other Rank: 76%
- Non-commissioned Officer: 19%
- Officer: 5%

Cause of Death

Everyone assumes that those who are recorded on memorials across the country were all killed in action. Whilst this was the case for the majority of Bidford's fatalities, others died of the result of their wounds, through illness or accidents. A breakdown of the cause of death of the men from Bidford gives us a good insight.

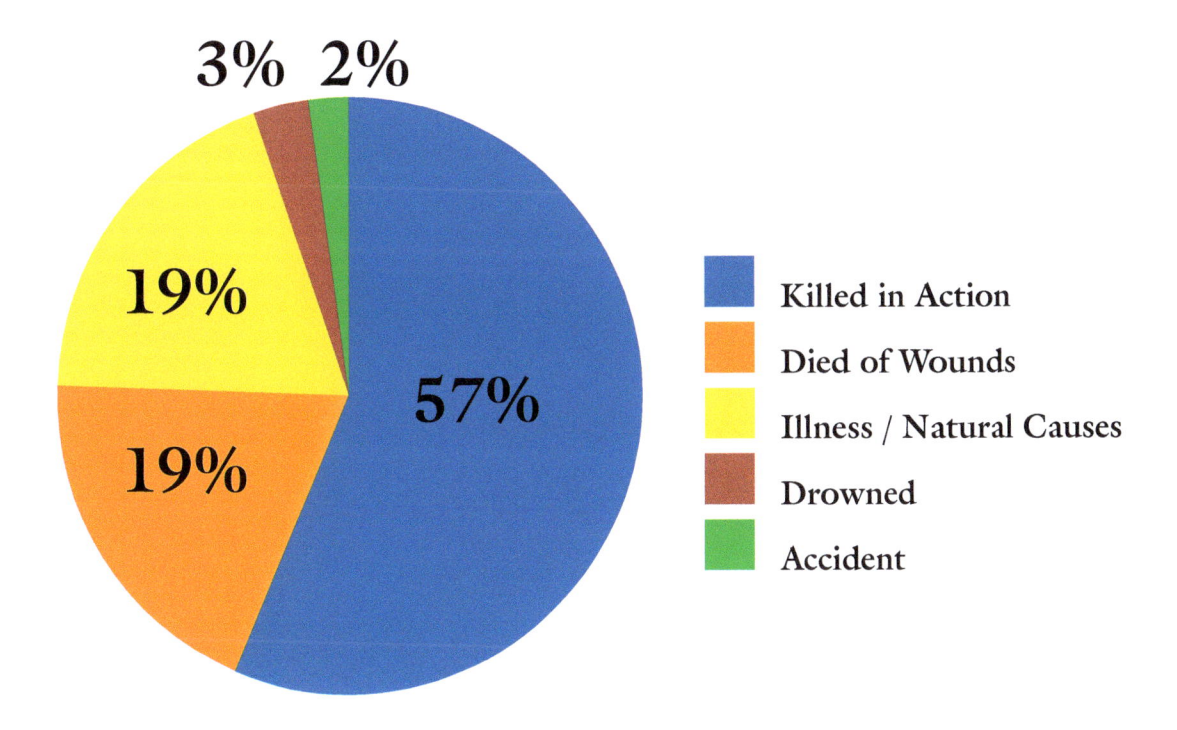

- Killed in Action: 57%
- Died of Wounds: 19%
- Illness / Natural Causes: 19%
- Drowned: 3%
- Accident: 2%

We need to remember, however, that whatever the cause of death, it was as a result of serving their country in the Great War and there should be no distinction between them.

Bibliography

- The Warwickshire Regimental Museum (Battalion Diaries)
- The Worcestershire Regimental Museum (Battalion Diaries)
- The Grenadier Guards Museum (Battalion Diaries)
- The Commonwealth War Graves Commission (cemetery details and pictures)
- Canadian Army Records (Leacroft Freer and Frank Hancock)
- Evesham Journal Archives (Records, 1914-19)
- The National Archives, Kew
- De Ruvigny Roll of Honour
- Warwickshire Records Office (Bidford School logbook, 1914, 1916, 1917)
- 1891, 1901, 1911 Census records
- Ensor, 'England, 1870-1914'
- A. N. Wilson,' The Victorians'
- Bidford-on-Avon Parish Magazines:
  December 1899, February, March, June 1900 editions

Interviews completed by Bob Marshall with the following:

- Mona Arrowsmith   re: Charles Heaver
- Donald Mayrick   re: Tom Mayrick
- Joan McCrorie   re: Fred McQuay
- Bill Russell

# WE WILL REMEMBER THEM
INDEX

Fatalities named on the Bidford War Memorial are highlighted in bold
Locations of the war dead can be found under Cemeteries and Memorials

Alcester	25, 66, 71, 84, 90	- High Wood	63
	100, 106, 116, 137, 149, 151, 153	- Hooge	21, 58, 95
Armistice	136, 137, 157	- Kimberley	3, 10
Ash, Ernest	16, **104**, 106	- Ladysmith	3, 6
Baden Powell, Robert	6	- Le Catauea	23
Barton	32, 37, 40, 64, 96	- Loos	23, 49, 120
	98, 118, 134, 138, 142	- Mafeking	3, 6
Bapaume	53	- Mons	14, 20, 23, 43, 100, 110, 160
Bennett, Frederick Mark	100	- Neuve Chappelle	23
Bennett, William Rogers	80	- Passchendaele	79, 102, 104, 116
Battles:		- Paardeberg	7-8
- Aisne	124	- Polygon Wood	104
- Arras	14, 79, 87, 88, 95, 98,	- Scarpe	87, 116, 147
	101, 112, 116, 134, 147	- Somme	14, 38, 53, 56, 59-60, 64, 69-70
- Aubers Ridge	23		74-75, 79, 81, 86, 88-89, 95, 98, 101, 108, 116, 145
- Belewarde Lake	33	- Spion Kop	3
- Bloemfontein	6-9	- Vimy Ridge	31, 59, 622, 143
- Broodseinde	104, 107	- Ypres	14, 20, 23, 25, 28, 33, 35
- Cambrai	79, 108, 112		37, 54, 79, 80, 101, 104, 107, 111
- Colesburg	9		112, 116, 118, 123, 128, 147
- Delville Wood	64, 81, 95, 116	**Beard, Alfred Henry**	118
- Gallipoli	14, 23, 29-30, 40, 44, 83	Beaumont-Hamel	74-75
	89, 98, 108, 137	Bethune	47, 60, 74, 101, 120
- Gheluvelt	21	Bickmarsh	17, 108, 112, 120

171

"We Will Remember Them"

Bidford:
- Bell Court   *5, 157*
- Bull's Head Pub   *34*
- Coronation Row   *17, 68*
- Falcon Buildings   *84, 86, 116, 124*
- Icknield Street   *26, 68, 145*
- Salford Road   *17, 29, 30, 34, 42, 44, 46, 70 100, 104, 110, 122, 140*
- Tower Hill   *48, 50, 54, 58, 68, 106 128, 136, 157*
- War Memorial   *158-161*
- White Lion Hotel   *7, 14, 71, 149*

Birmingham Daily Post   *93*
Blackwell, Samuel Frederick Baker *108*
Bott, William   *31, 98*
British Expeditionary Force   *20, 130*

Cemeteries:
- Adanac   *128, 129*
- Bac-du-Sud   *118*
- Bettrichies   *136*
- Bidford (St. Laurence)   *26, 71, 72, 84, 108, 140, 145*
- Boulogne Eastern   *48-49*
- Delville Wood   *64, 81, 95, 116*
- Doiran   *91*
- Etaples   *81*
- Feuchy Chapel   *146*
- Harlebeke   *101*
- Hermies Hill   *134*
- Kantara   *82-83*
- La Targette   *100*
- La Neuville   *68*
- Les Boeufs (Guards)   *80*
- Le Treport   *66-67, 134*
- Lijssenhoek   *54*
- Mendingham   *122-123*
- Mericourt-le-Abbe   *56*
- Montescourt-Lizerolles   *116-117*
- Oxford Road, Ypres   *102*
- Ribecourt   *108-109*
- St Sever   *26*
- Sophia, Bulgaria   *138*
- Sucrerie   *38*
- Sunken Road, Viller-Plouich   *112*
- Valenciennes   *132-133*
- Varennes   *76*
- White House, St Jean-les-Ypres   *106*

Choques   *46-47*
Churchley, Samuel   *17, 102*
Cleeve Prior   *110, 151*
Collett, Albert   *17, 68*
Contalmaison   *56-57*
Crawford, Dr   *160*
Dance, Philip   *126-127*
Dee, Edward George   *64*
Davis, Frank   *115, 145*
Davis, Herbert Leonard   *58-59, 128*
Davis, W. H. - Sculptor   *160*
Distinguished Conduct Medal   *66, 74*
Dorsington   *96*
Edkins, Christopher John   *74*
Egypt   *82-83, 98*
Evans, Reverend Alfred   *3*
Evans, Reverend J. W.   *14, 71*
Evesham Journal   *5, 7, 9, 16, 61, 87, 149 151, 153, 152, 154, 157, 160*
Festubert   *60, 74*
Finnemore, Michael   *101*

172

Index

Fosbroke G.H., Dr	*5, 14, 27*
Freeman, Ben	*4, 8*
Freeman, William Henry (Harry)	**34**
Freer, Leacroft Howard	*31, 32, 108, 170*
Gardner, David	*72*
Gould, Gerald	*16, 115, 136-137*
Givenchy	*32, 49*
Gully Beach	*41, 44*
Gully Ravine	*40, 41*
Hancock, Harry	*4, 115, 142-143*
Hancocks, Frank	*92-93*
Harris, Edgar	*17, 33, 35*
Harris, T	*4, 10, 164*
Hartland, Arthur	*60, 95*
Hartwell, Horace	**88**
Heaver, Charles	*17, 132, 170*
Holder:	
- George	*7*
- Mrs	*5*
Houghton, Bernard	*89*
Houghton, Mr	*153*
Hughes, Richard	*76*
Kitchener, General	*14, 17, 23, 49, 53, 86*
Leamington	*29, 40, 71*
Langemarck	*105, 111, 16*
Lane, William George	*56*
Le Havre	*27, 42, 43, 106, 134, 138*
Lemurhoch	*25*
Leonard, George	*66, 84*
Liddell, Francis	*120*
Liddell, William Henry	*112*
Locke:	
- George	*110, 164*
- Henry	*4, 110, 160, 164*
- **Nathan**	*110*
- William	*164*
Longueval	*63, 64, 69, 70*
Marlcliff	*14, 20, 101, 126*
Mayrick, Thomas	*69, 70*
McQuay, Fred	*62*
Memorials:	
- Arras	*86, 88, 94, 96, 146*
- Helles	*29, 30, 40, 41*
- Loos	*120*
- Menin Gate	*25, 27, 28, 33, 34, 35, 37*
- Thiepval	*58, 60, 61, 62, 89*
- Tyne Cot	*104, 110*
- Vimy Ridge	*31, 39, 92*
Military Medal	*153*
Millward, Thomas William	*122*
Moore, Jesse	*153, 165*
Nichols, Harry	*20*
Nutting, Phil	*4, 10, 165*
Oakey, George	*134-135*
Oversley	*25, 38*
Payne, William John Henry	*96*
Pitcher, Bernard	*86*
Pitcher, Carl	*124*
Poperinghe, casualty clearing station	*14, 21*
Fosbroke-Power, George Henry	*27*
Power, Sir D'Arcy	*27*
Pulham, Cecil Raymond	*116*
Pulham, William Francis	*84, 115*
Quiney, J	*4, 9*
Reeves, Norman Chester	*82*
Regiments:	
- Canadian Expeditionary Force	*31, 32, 168*
- Coldstream Guards	*4, 10, 42, 164, 168*

173

- Dorset Regiment	80, 153, 168	**Rose, Leonard Sylvester**	115, 140
- Essex Regiment	45, 88, 164, 168	**Round, Edward**	146
- Gloucestershire Regiment	112, 142, 168	Rouen	26, 81, 122
- Grenadier Guards	134, 165, 168, 170	Russell, Bill	17, 19, 170
- Hampshire Regiment	44, 98, 120, 168	**Russell, Reginald**	128
- King's Hussars	100, 168	**Russell, Thomas Albert**	48
- King's Royal Rifles Corps	4, 46, 64, 101, 116, 142	Salford Priors	25, 82, 100, 122, 130, 145
- Lincolnshire Regiment	33, 168	**Seymour, John**	42
- Machine Gun Corps	104, 115, 116, 164, 165, 186	**Sheasby, Edwin**	26
- Middlesex Regiment	27, 168	**Smith, Frederick George**	90
- Norfolk Regiment	108, 168	**Smith, John Corbett**	50
- Oxford and Bucks Light Infantry	48, 60, 74, 88, 90, 94, 98, 118, 136, 138, 168	Smith, Tom	150
		Spanbrockmolen	25
- Royal Air Force	130, 168	Spittle, Albert	4, 7, 8
- Royal Army Service Corps	72, 164, 168	**Stanford, Louis**	17, 94
- Royal Berkshire Regiment	110, 168	Survivors – see list on pages	162 - 165
- Royal Engineers	45, 82, 102, 122, 140, 168	**Tarrant, Frederick**	17, 29
- Royal Field Artillery	54, 88, 126, 163, 165, 168	**Taylor, Thomas Henry**	37
		Taylor, Walter William	37, 98
- Royal Flying Corps	71, 76, 130, 164, 168	Transvaal	3, 100
- Royal Garrison Artillery	26, 106, 163, 164, 168	United Patriots National Benefit Society	5
- Royal Marine Light Infantry	132, 168	Victoria Cross	30, 45
- Royal Rifles Field Force	10	Wesson, T	4
- Royal Warwickshire Regiment	38, 50, 62, 68, 70, 71, 86, 96, 110, 115, 134, 136, 160, 168	**Wheatley, Henry John (Harry)**	24
		Wilcox, Harry	4, 10
- South Staffordshire Regiment	66, 168	**Wilkes, Christopher John Samuel**	130
- Wiltshire Regiment	90, 124, 168	Wilson, E. A.	5, 11
- Worcestershire Regiment	20, 24-25, 29, 34, 40, 56-57, 58-59, 89, 146-147, 163-164, 168, 170	**Woodhouse, William**	106
		Worcester	17, 20, 24, 25, 34, 58, 89, 138
Richardson, Thomas	25	**Wright, Frederick**	40
Roberts, General	3, 7	**Wright, George Benjamin**	138
Rose, Arthur	46	Zillebeke	21
		Zonebeke	29